NAKED SALSA

A look at marriage and parenthood through the naked eye

Crystal Henry

Naked Salsa – Volume I Copyright© 2014 by Crystal Henry
Cover Art Copyright© 2014 by Crystal Henry

Columns previously published in *Our Town* magazine, ScaryMommy.com, preschoolproblems.blogspot.com and HerEggsMyBasket.blogspot.com

No part of this book may be reproduced or transmitted in any form or by any means, electronic or mechanical including photocopying, recording or by any information storage and retrieval system, without permission from the copyright owner.
ISBN-13: 978-1500605889

For my Sunshine and Sweet Pea. You are my messy but hilarious inspiration and the greatest thing that has ever come from me being naked.

Acknowledgments

I would first like to thank my wonderfully forgiving editors, Patricia Camburn Zick (http://www.pczick.com) and Albert Isaac (http://authorsden.com/AlbertLIsaac). They are the two most inspiring writers in my life, and they've both put up with a lot of my crap. Pat is a phenomenal author whose expertise helped guide me throughout my writing career. Plus she gave me my first writing gig, and I will forever be indebted to her for that. Albert is my sounding board and inspiration. He's a writer to the very core, and his passion inspires me. I'm proud to know him as an editor and as a friend. They are both masters of the craft, and they not only give me something to strive for, but they help and encourage me on my own writing journey. So to them I say thank you. Thank you for giving me a shot, and thanks for not firing me when I blew deadlines faster than a Vegas hooker.

I'd also like to thank my family. My childhood with Aunt Lovie was always fueled by imagination and creativity. Not every child had an activity book made out of newspaper comic cut-outs. Then there's my brother Tyler, who has always been so unwaveringly supportive, even though he spent most of his childhood as my girl dog Lisa. And of course I have to thank my Nana and Papaw: my most loyal readers who weren't being paid to read my stuff. Thanks for hanging in there. Then there's my mother-in-law. I have to thank Marie for being such a good sport. I poke fun at her clean freakiness, but it's all in good fun. I'm so happy to call her my mother-in-love and my friend.

Finally I'd like to thank my two biggest fans. My mother and my husband are at the absolute opposite ends of the spectrum on most issues, but one thing they've always been united on is their steadfast support for my craft.

My mother has been my loudest cheerleader since I could read my first word, which she claims was at 2 years old. She might be the biggest liar in the world, but she has always pushed me to reach farther and dream bigger than I ever imagined possible.

Then there's my Hubs. The most practical black-and-white thinking engineer on the face of the planet, and yet he whole-heartedly encourages me to chase my dreams. He is the honest voice I need to balance out my mother's rose colored praises. He is my voice of reason while also being my vote of confidence. They are the yin and the yang of my writing success.

I will forever be grateful to these people who have helped shaped who I am, and who are the very inspiration for my writing.

This book is for you.

Why Hello There...Shall We Get Naked?

Getting naked means different things throughout life. We come into the world naked, and our views go from innocence to modesty to curiosity.

Before marriage naked is forbidden, but enticing. And even after taking the plunge into commitment, naked is new and full of exploration. In the early days of marriage it is still secretive and thrilling. It's reserved for a midday romp or the occasional glimpse as it disappears behind a shower curtain. It's an elusive naked. And it is good.

If you stay naked long enough it can lead to a new kind of naked. Husbands who have only seen their wives naked in a sexual way will see them naked in a new setting. Sweaty and primal, they grunt and push their naked offspring into the world. This naked is raw and real and scary and beautiful and disgusting. But it is still a good naked.

Once the naked is multiplied it changes once again. There are naked breasts feeding babies all over town. Hungry babies don't have a problem with naked boobs in Chili's. They can't exactly munch on a Triple Dipper, so they make do. Then naked little butts run around spilling and squishing and drawing and messing. Your once naked walls and floors are covered in boogers and crayons and jelly. This naked is a very different naked than the early days of marriage, but it is still a good naked. It's a naked that reminds you why you got naked together in the first place. Speaking of that kind of naked, it rarely happens anymore.

As the little naked butts start to put on underwear and cover their asses so to speak, the sexy naked makes a come-back. It's not as new as it once was, but it's like finding your first car on a used lot. There's some nostalgia in this naked, and although there are some dents and scratches in it…it's still a good naked.

My first column was born a decade ago in a bar in Gainesville, Florida over a basket of chips and salsa. I was a newlywed journalism student swapping funny stories with my fellow writers and my then editor, Pat.

I told Pat a story about losing a bet with my Hubs where I ended up making a batch of salsa wearing nothing but tube socks. We were all dying laughing, and she said in passing that I should write a column in our magazine about this stuff. It stuck in my head, and I got the courage a few days later to ask her if she was serious in her offer.

She said she was, and after I picked myself up off the floor we talked about the title for my new column about married life. I jokingly said, "What if we called it Naked Salsa?" We both laughed and tossed around a few more titles, but that one just stuck. It was a little racy for the family magazine we worked for, but it was the most fitting.

At first the idea of my own column was both terrifying and invigorating. I couldn't imagine that anyone would want to read what I had to say, and I was afraid I would run out of material. But Naked Salsa was more than indecent culinary skills. It was about putting myself out there and being vulnerable. And I quickly found out, married life is anything but dull. The material wrote itself.

My column has evolved over the years from a snarky account of newlywed life to a reflective narrative on parenting. But the intention has been and always will be to give insight into the ridiculous journey that is life in the most honest and humorous way.

And the best way I saw to simultaneously be honest and have a few laughs was for me to just get Naked.

Cheeseburger in Paradise

I love a good greasy cheeseburger. One cooked fresh on a griddle, so that the meat is nice and juicy and the bun is soft. A good sign is when they are served wrapped in wax paper, and the grease soaks through the paper sack. When I think about that melted cheese hugging the savory burger to the bun, my saliva glands explode and I think, "Mmm I could eat that every day." The third grader in me says, "If you love it so much, why don't you marry it?"

Aside from the fact that I am already happily married, and the fact that I think it is illegal in most states, that silly little rhetoric brings up an interesting point. Being married is like buying the restaurant that serves your favorite meal.

When Cary and I were dating it was just fun. We laughed all the time, ogled each other's physiques and went on spontaneous camping trips to the beach whenever the mood struck us. It was a blast, and I thought, "I want to spend every second of every day with this guy." I wanted that cheeseburger for breakfast, lunch and dinner. But it takes more than inside jokes, camping trips and a cute butt to make a relationship last. Eventually cheeseburgers three times a day will give you a little heartburn. So we started having little spats here and there. I was grouchy after work, or he wanted to watch baseball when The Notebook was on. But it was nothing a night out and a little extra cuddling wouldn't fix. So we took a couple Tums now and then and it was fine. I still wanted that cheeseburger. And my milkshake must not have been too bad either, because before I knew it he was down on one knee asking to buy the restaurant.

In August of 2004 I sold off my freedom for a down payment on Cary's Burger Palace. But as any good business owner knows, you have to put in a lot of face time if you want your restaurant to succeed. After all over 50 percent of new businesses fail in the first year, and only a little less than 50 percent of marriages fail over time. So it was a cheeseburger life morning, noon and night. But it was good because it was new and exciting. It was the beginning of our adventure together.

But as every business owner also knows that the first year is the hardest. And it was. There was a lot about the restaurant business I had to adjust to. The kitchen had a few fires, there were issues with the dishwasher and the books were a little harder to manage than I'd anticipated. But we made it through, and despite the setbacks we profited.

A few years went by and my life was full of that yummy cheesy goodness. There was Meaty Monday through Sizzlin' Sunday of burger after burger after burger. I woke up to cheeseburgers in the morning, I had them for lunch, and I kissed their buns each night before bed. Naturally I put on a few pounds, and he went from being a Quarter Pounder to a Big Mac, but we were happy. However, when you have the same thing day after day after day it starts to get a little well…bland.

Now don't get me wrong, I still loved cheeseburgers. But it was time to spice it up. So we introduced some date night jalapenos, pepper jack kisses and some hickory smoked bacon vacations, and it was jalapeno bacon cheeseburger paradise.

My burger buddy and I have been through a lot over the past five years. Sometimes the meat has a little gristle or the busboy forgets to take out the trash. But we're still open for business. And now that we have our small fry, I feel like business is booming. She adds a whole new perspective on my life, and makes me realize why I bought the Burger Palace to begin with. Sure she adds to the workload. I had to switch from being open until 10 p.m. to being a 24-hour drive thru. But that 4 a.m. feeding proves to be a good time to catch up on my writing.

And in the quiet of the early hours, as I look at my little small fry curled up next to that cheeseburger, I know that all the work I do is worth it. Just like that restaurant owner, I know I have to put in a full day if I want to succeed. The second you stop working at it, you might as well board up the windows. You can't coast through, and you can't let someone else do all the work. It's hard and at times it gets downright dirty. But I am happy to report that despite the mountain of dishes, heartburn and occasional cranky customer, at the end of the day I can just curl up with my cheeseburger and say, "I love my job."

My Boobs: An Exposé

This column was submitted to the Our Town Magazine, but we thought it showed a little too much nip for a family publication.

When I was 9 years old my mother said something horrible to me. "Crystal," she said. "It's time for a bra."

What a horrible thing to say to a 9 year old. I liked building forts and climbing trees. There was no room for a bra in the wilderness. I was going into Level 3 in gymnastics. How did she expect that bra to fit into my leotard? There was barely enough room in there as it was, especially with those oh-so-inconvenient little anthills that just cropped up on my chest overnight.

But sadly, she was right and I've been sporting an over the shoulder boulder holder since the 4th grade. The first day was uncomfortable, but no one seemed to notice my new accessory. No, it wasn't until the next week in the lunch line that Jacob Nichol noticed my strap peeking out of my shirt. That sweet little darling grabbed the clasp of my 24AA, pulled back and let her rip. He giggled hysterically as the strap smacked me in the back. I whirled around and screamed at him to cut it out, which got me a stern look from the teacher on lunch duty.

But Jacob didn't quit. He kept snapping my bra strap out on the playground until I had a bright red welt on my back. I tried running away, but he was a quick little sucker. I tried to tell the coach, but I was told just to ignore him because "boys will be boys."

Well that may be, but girls will be girls too. So I took matters into my own hands. I coaxed Jacob under the slide by telling him that I would show him my bra. He took the bait, and as soon as he was under the slide and out of the coach's sight, I planted my foot right between his legs. Jacob lost his interest in my bra that day, and probably all other bras for the rest of his life judging by the force behind my foot. It was then that I realized the strange fascination that people have with these puppies and the power that comes with their mysticism.

I truly don't understand it. They're just boobs. They are mounds of fat, muscle, breast tissue, and a few milk ducts. What's the big deal?

But they are a very big deal in our society. Men pay big bucks to see them, and women pay big bucks to have them. For some reason people find the human mammary glands to be incredibly fascinating. I doubt a bull would walk by a cow and ogle her udders. And I doubt any sows would give their pigtails to have bigger teats. But for some reason human boobs are quite the hot commodity.

I've found this obsession to be magnified now that I'm a nursing mother. I have the disgusting habit of feeding my child in public, and people have not been shy to let me know how horrifying this display of my sweater puppets really is.

Now, in high school I could have sold tickets to see the twins. Step right up ladies and gents to see the eighth and ninth wonders of the world – a woman's breasts. Whoopee. A friend of mine in high school even had names for them. Helga and Olga were big celebrities in their prime. But now that they are functional, and I am using them to sustain human life as per their original design, I am often shunned by society. No one likes a pair of workin' boobs.

I would love to have this explained to me because I'm not sure at what point my cha-chas transform into frightening Gila monsters bent on world domination. I can wear a low cut top, and I'm ok. No one is concerned that one of the girls will jump out and yell "Boo." But the second I unsnap the nursing tank, I am an exhibitionist and should be thrown in the stocks.

I thought maybe the nipple was the offending party. But that can't be because I have seen more than one fat guy walking down the beach with a D cup and pepperoni nipples. No one tosses him his sleeveless tank to slip on, so I know that can't be it. Plus because of divine design, my nip is covered by the baby's mouth while she's nursing. So I guess the offensive part must be the breast itself.

But where does it get offensive? It's the same skin that is on my neck or my arm. Is it the fat under the skin? Is it the milk ducts? I just don't get what is so horrid about the breast that I can't just feed my kid in public without getting a disgusted look or huff.

People constantly tell me they are supportive of my decision to nurse, but it is a private moment that should only be shared at home. Well tell that to my screaming baby when she gets hungry at Chili's. Should I be a shut-in until the child is weaned? I don't think so as long as long as Pepperoni Pete is still wandering the beaches of the Atlantic coast.

And then there are those progressive types that are supportive of my decision to nurse as long as I wear one of those trendy Udder Covers. Well that's all fine and good for those mommies with calm and peaceful nursers. But as the two people who read my column know, this kid has been as active as a feral cat in a burlap sack since she was in utero. So trying to keep a nursing cover over her head while she eats is an Olympic sport that I just am not trained for. I tend to draw less attention if I just discreetly whip it out than if I try to cover her up and then wrestle her arms while she tries to claw her way to freedom.

It's not like I'm wearing tassels and slinking up and down a pole. I'm feeding my child. If my boobs could talk they would say, "Nothing to see here folks. Just doing my job."

So I developed a little trick for people to help them avoid seeing the disgusting display I put on each time my offspring needs nourishment. Take your chin and point it in the opposite direction of my breasts. If my calculations are correct this should take me out of your line of sight. If your neck muscles are not yet strong enough for this pose, try taking your left eyelid and bringing it down over your left eyeball. Repeat on the right side.

This should take care of the problem, but if it doesn't my advice is to get over it and just embrace my boobs for the magnificently functional wonders that they are.

Honey Mooners

This was the very first column I ever wrote for Our Town Magazine

There are several theories about the origin of the honeymoon. Some say in ancient times when a man decided to tie the knot, he would often take the unwilling woman to a hidden place where her relatives could not find them. They would drink a honey brew and hide until the moon completed its phases.

Others say the word honeymoon first appeared in the 16th century in reference to the sweetness of a new marriage. The moon served as a bitter reminder that the sweetness of the marriage, like a full moon, would not last forever.

Nowadays people refer to the "honeymoon phase" as a blissful period of lounging on beds of rainbows and kisses with your new spouse.

All I have to say is thank God the honeymoon is over.

Don't get me wrong, I love my husband. And not a day goes by that I don't thank my lucky stars I found that special someone to chauffeur me around town on a quest for just the right kind of cookies and cream. But if I had to stay in the honeymoon phase of our marriage for the rest of my life, I just might kill him.

If there was an award in high school for least likely to get married before turning 40, I would have won by a landslide. The same week I unwittingly met my future husband, my good friend from high school called to tell me she was getting engaged, and I repeatedly told her she was too young for all that nonsense.

Less than a year later I was standing beside her at a wedding during one of the most beautiful West Texas sunsets in history. Oddly enough I was in the wedding gown and she was standing in the ugly purple bridesmaid dress.

The wedding went off without a hitch, which at the time seemed like a good omen for the honeymoon phase to follow.

It wasn't.

I described this period of the marriage like living on a big moon made of golden-sweet honey, which sounds good until you discover that a giant honey-loving grizzly bear also lives there. And the honey has you stuck firmly to the ground with no escape. Not to mention this particular bear leaves his toenails on the coffee table and has a problem with you leaving laundry in the basket for a week.

To be nice about it there were times I thought about setting a bear trap for my new husband. Why weren't we canoodling in bed all Sunday morning after staying up talking about our dreams all Saturday night?

Naturally there had to be something wrong with him. There was no way that I was difficult to live with.

So we fought. And we fought.

Our fights ranged anywhere from "Did you seriously just sit at home all day and do nothing while I was at work?" to "Uh huh, and who is Nikki Sue again?" We would battle it out well into the night until one of us passed out from exhaustion. But as sure as a bear loves honey we would be at it again the very next day. We were at our wits end and ready to throw in the towel. This was all supposed to be so easy. We were in the honeymoon phase for crying out loud.

Finally when my vocal chords couldn't take the yelling anymore I turned to sweet revenge. One day after a fight my foe headed down to the garage and my plan was launched. I hollowed out his pint of Rocky Road and added a generous amount of Louisiana hot sauce. I patched the treat, returned it to the freezer and waited.

Each time that week when my hubby started in, I just looked at him and smiled, knowing that soon he would discover my revenge a la mode. I think that simple act may have ended our honeymoon and kick started our marriage.

The look on his face when he gulped down the first bite of the sabotaged sweet was worth all the arguments and late night scream fests. He spiked the pint into the trashcan and chucked the spoon into the sink. But as he rounded the corner to scold me, I was laughing too hard for him to continue.

It was then that I realized that we were taking this whole marriage thing too seriously. It takes time to develop a strong marriage, but we were naïve enough to think it would happen overnight.

So my advice to all the newlyweds this June is to forget about that honey-sweet idea you have about marriage. Instead cherish those rocky roads you travel together. Your marriage wouldn't be as spicy without them.

And remember, it only gets sweeter once the honeymoon is over.

Life is What Happens When You're Busy Making Plans

My life is rapidly changing. My husband got a job in a new city, so we are packing up and moving to small-town Indiana. Along with that we decided to have a baby, buy a new car and a new house. It's all so wonderfully scary and exciting. Yet all these things are plans that we've made. Things we could see coming and things we chose to do. They're decisions and choices that we have made. It is just recently that I've realized that life's choices are so often out of our control.

Everything started with the job hunt. Hubby found the perfect job with great pay and benefits. Everything was perfect, until I realized it was in Columbus, Indiana. Ugh. The mere thought of moving north after growing up in the South made me nauseous. I just knew I would hate the Yankee town and was planning our move out of Columbus before even thinking about the move in. But fine, if that's what we had to do I'd suck it up.

Then came the baby news. Just hours after finishing my last column about trying to get pregnant I found out we'd already succeeded. That was the happiest moment from a little pink line I've ever experienced. I couldn't hold it in and told everyone in my family, my friends at work and pretty much anyone who made eye contact (and sometimes even those who didn't).

It was perfect, and everything was falling into place. I quit caffeine, lunch meat and soft cheese. Our family sent tiny yellow booties and soft Winnie the Pooh blankets. I read pregnancy books cover to cover. I started tracking the baby's size in relation to food. One week it was a poppy seed, and then it was a blueberry.

I experienced the joys of pregnancy from morning sickness to backaches. I was on cloud nine. The suspense of my 12-week check-up was almost too much to handle because we were going to hear the heartbeat of our first little baby.

And then came the choices again. We found out through an ultrasound that we were expecting twins, but something was wrong. I just knew it. Those little peanuts on the ultrasound screen were too small to be my babies.

My heart stopped as the transducer ran through the cold gel on my tummy.

They were supposed to be limes or plums, not peanuts. The ultrasound tech got quiet, but she didn't need to say it. I'd been watching other 12-week ultrasounds online, and I knew what I should have seen. My babies had died four weeks ago. I lost them.

But in keeping with the rest of my life, this was another choice I would make. Since I hadn't actually miscarried them I got the ghastly privilege of deciding how I would rid my womb of those precious little ones. There was no convincing the rest of my body to take care of it. As far as my hormones were concerned I was still pregnant, morning sickness and all.

Ahh, choices. Well that's what life is all about right? I waited a week, had a second confirming ultrasound and went ahead with a D&C.

I just recovered from surgery in time to make the trip to Indiana to find a house. This was going to be a bright choice in the midst of such dark ones. We sent the Realtor a list of about 30 houses we wanted to tackle in one weekend. Surely we would find our house with all those choices.

We put in a full 12-hour day of house hunting, and found the one for us on McClennan Court. It had a few things that I would have changed, but the Realtor got a call informing us that the seller was motivated and needed to sell the house quickly. Since we would be moving in less than two months, we were motivated to buy it quickly.

We put a bid in at 8:30 that night, expecting to hear back the next day by 5 p.m. We spent the next day scoping out the area, and as much as I fought it I was actually starting to really like the town. Maybe it wouldn't be so bad living in the Midwest. It had all the comforts of a big city without any of the downsides. Plus we had a great house picked out. All was right with the world.

The Realtor called at 4:30 with the news, just 24 hours before we were to fly back home. The seller declined our offer, refusing to take less than asking price and requiring us to pay taxes on the property for the year she owned it. We panicked.

These choices were just backfiring one after another. We scrambled that night to find some houses to look at before we flew out the next day. There was no time or money to make another house-hunting trip, and our Realtor was in Indianapolis with another client. We were screwed. We looked at one horrid house that night, and got one potential house scheduled for the next morning.

I hardly slept that night. I just laid there wondering why it seemed that nothing could go right in my life. I would be moving away from my home with the people and places I loved. I had no baby and now no home. What did I do to deserve this? These weren't the choices I made. My plans took me to a beautiful home in the South surrounded by family and friends who would ooh and ahh over my brand new baby. What was this pile of crap I stepped in?

I was still pouting when we pulled up to the house the next morning. The Realtor was late, but whatever. We looked at 30 houses the day before and the only one we wanted wasn't happening. I knew there was no way this one house would be it.

But then it was.

I have never been so happy to be so wrong in my life. It was my house. I knew it when I walked in. I could see us snuggling in front of the cozy fireplace and cooking Thanksgiving dinner in my dream kitchen. I was home. It only took a few hours for the sellers to accept our offer. We agreed on the asking price, so it was an easy choice for them.

As we sat in the airport gushing about which bedroom to turn into a nursery, I realized what a beautiful disaster my life really is. I got a house I didn't ask for in a town I didn't ask for. But both were exactly what I wanted. And the same will be for our children. I firmly believe we get the children we're supposed to have, and as I said in my last column, I'll get mine all in due time. I've realized it's not my choice to make.

Each time I think I'm in control, the rug is ripped from under me and I tumble into reality. Call it God or fate or whatever you want, but there is a plan for our lives. We can stress over the choices we face, but for better or worse they aren't always ours to make. And that's the beauty of it.

Some of the greatest gifts I've ever been given weren't on my list. I'm so lucky that life doesn't treat me like a spoiled child who gets everything she wants. And I think next time I don't get my way, I won't kick and scream and throw a tantrum. I'll just wait and see what better choice is waiting just around the corner.

Kidnapped

On a still evening in June, at 7:53 p.m., I was kidnapped. My whole world was turned upside down by someone I'd never met, and I am now forced to bend to my captor's every will. If her demands are not met, I pay dearly. And she releases a fury I have never known.

To the untrained eye it would seem I could easily escape this hijacker. After all I outweigh her by about 140 pounds, and she isn't exactly able to chase me down or even walk for that matter. She can't really see that well, and she doesn't even speak English. So should I want to call for help, she wouldn't know what I was saying as long as I used a silly or sweet tone of voice.

However, ever since that fateful night in June, I have been a slave to this tiny controller. I am forced to prepare all of her meals, do all of her laundry, and she expects me to read her mind. I haven't slept in weeks, and the amount of excrement I'm expected to handle is shocking.

It's madness. Sometimes I go days without stepping foot outside. When I do go out I know it's only a matter of time before she starts barking orders.

Still, I suppose I may have developed Stockholm syndrome. This psychological condition is seen in abducted hostages sometimes, and the captives become emotionally attached to their captors. And I have to admit that I have become quite emotionally involved with this little tyrant. She can scream at me because I clumsily dropped her blanket, or demand that I do laps around the house. And yet as soon as she cracks a tiny grin, even though it's probably just gas, I realize I would readily take a bullet for this girl.

Still it's not easy being ordered around like this. The day before I was captured, life was different. I was free. When I wanted to sit down for lunch, I sat down for lunch. If I had to go to the bathroom, I went.

Now she dictates my lunch and potty breaks. I am only allowed to grab a quick bite for myself after her meal has been served and she is satisfied. My bathroom breaks are rushed, and if she allows me to take a shower I am grateful.

My husband comes to visit each night after he gets off work. And the little ruler is usually sleeping when he arrives. She'll sigh and smile sweetly to fool him into thinking this is her normal demeanor. And it seems I'm the only one who knows how demanding she has been all day.

Sometimes he'll play hero and restrain her for a few minutes so that I can use the bathroom or grab a quick bite of a cold meal I heated up at noon. And he's very proud of himself when he manages to lull her to sleep or keep her at bay. But he usually just falls asleep on the job, and I'm back in action as the servant to this tiny master.

And I think by now my former employer has come to realize that I've been taken, since I haven't been in to work in weeks. I laugh now as I remember a time when working until 7 p.m. was a long day. I feel that my life since my capture has turned into one very long day with short bursts of half sleep here and there. Getting off work at midnight would seem like a luxury now. But I don't. My new boss keeps me on call 24 hours a day, 7 days a week. And I have yet to see a paycheck.

But as I said, she has some sort of hold over me. I just can't bring myself to try and escape or even tell her no when she makes her demands. Friends and family have offered distract her and let me escape for a little while. But I can't even do that. She has me hypnotized and I can spend hours just sitting and watching her sleep.

So I guess for the time being I am a willing captive. I will offer myself to her when she is hungry. I'll run her bath and give her a massage when she requires it. I'll even entertain her and make up songs about her bodily functions just to please her. And maybe, just maybe, one day I will escape -- if she would just quit smiling at me.

Sweet Dreams

As a mother of an infant people often ask me the same three questions about my daughter.

Is she crawling? "Oh yes," I proudly reply. "She's even trying to walk."

Is she always this alert and friendly? "Oh goodness yes," I proudly report. "Since the day she was born."

And how is she sleeping? Gulp. "Through the night," I reply with a hint of guilt in my voice. And then I softly add "As long as she's in our bed."

This gets one of two reactions. The first is sheer horror. It's as if I just told them that she works nights in an underground puppy torture factory. I'm told what a huge mistake that is. I'll pay for it later. And oh I'll know better for the next one not to commit this heinous of all parenting crimes.

The second type of reaction is a shameful admission of their dirty little secret. They too did the unthinkable and co-slept with their child.

Now before I had a baby, I was on board with the first group. Knowing better than all those weak-willed ninnies with mommy rotten children, I smugly declared that my child would never ever under any circumstances no friggin' way not ever sleep in my bed. But then again, before I had a child, I said a lot of silly things.

A lot of people believe in the hocus pocus idea that your thoughts and verbalized wishes somehow control reality. For instance if you believe hard enough and say it often enough that you're going to get that promotion, it will happen. Well when it comes to parenting I've found that the harder you believe and the more you run your mouth about how things will be, the more words you have to eat. No wonder mom jeans were invented. You need some elastic high-waisted pants after all those I'll Nevers you have to choke down.

It's just so easy to judge and point fingers before you have a child. The rational thought that children who sleep with their parents will grow up to be clingy little mama's babies with no sense of independence got completely thrown out the window at 3 a.m. when my screaming infant stared up at me in wild-eyed abandonment.

And I know that I am sometimes viewed as a weak parent because I can't just let my baby cry in her room. It's supposedly good for her to learn to self soothe, and it's supposed to teach her independence. But there is nothing soothing about a baby who cries so hard she starts to choke and throw up. And I find it hard to believe that picking her up to calm her will cause her to hide under my skirt when she's 16 instead of cursing me under her breath when she's grounded for missing curfew.

No, the only cry-it-out method I am prepared to use at this point is one that involves a sappy chick flick I enjoy while nursing my daughter to sleep.

And some parents can get their kids to sleep alone. But it's not because they are a better parent than I am. It's because their child is different than my child. And it took me a while to get that.

My own mother said as a baby I didn't want to sleep in her room. Her movement woke me up, and I just slept better alone. And my dear mother-in-law reminds me all the time that her son slept by himself through the night a mere two weeks after she brought him home. Well lah tee friggin' dah. That's all fine and well if your child will do that. More power to you, and I encourage that behavior if it works for all involved. But my child is different.

Since day one, she had a very sensitive startle reflex. She would easily fall asleep, but the second she was laid down in her crib she would flail her arms and wake up screaming. Yes I tried swaddling. I all but put a strait jacket on the child. Yes I tried the wedge. I tried letting her fall asleep in her crib. I tried rocking her and then putting her down. I tried music. I tried no music. I tried shushing and patting and singing and nursing and bathing and reading and staying and leaving. Nothing worked.

The first night we brought her home, my husband laid her in her crib, and she started to cry. He came back into the bedroom, and I looked at him like he had a horn growing out of his nose. How could he just leave her in there alone and crying?

His rationale was that she was fed, her diaper was clean, and she needed to sleep in her bed. There was no reason for her to be upset. She was just trying to manipulate us. My first instinct was to punch him in the forehead, but I knew that we needed to stick together when it came to parenting. So I tried to ride it out. After laying there for about three minutes in tears the crying stopped, on her end at least. I crept down the hall and peeked in the room only to discover that my mother had come to her rescue.

"Don't just let this baby cry like that," she pleaded as she rocked and soothed her firstborn grandbaby.

"Mother," I said sternly in my very best responsible and controlled voice. "Put her down. We're parenting."

I swear she snickered at me in the dark, and I laugh now at how ridiculous I must have sounded. Because nine months later, as I sit here savoring the victory that she is napping in her crib, I realize that letting her sleep in my bed is what is best for us as a family. She sleeps, therefore we all sleep. I love waking up to her sweet little face, and my husband gets that extra time with her each morning and each night. She's learning that she can count on me to be there for her, and that night time is not a scary time, but rather a relaxing and peaceful time to recharge. She grows so fast each day, and I know one day she might not want to give me a kiss in front of her friends. So for now, I'm going to enjoy the closeness we share and go on letting her sleep next to me.

Judge me all you want. But I'm parenting.

Vacation Tips from my 4-year-old
Originally published on scarymommy.com and preschoolproblems.blogspot.com

Mom and Dad keep dragging me to this rat hole they call Disney World. They get all stupid excited over it so I play along. But by the last day I'm kinda over their B.S. So here are some travel tips for your final day of vacation.

1. Mom and Pop should be rested at this point. They've had an entire week of dragging us around the theme parks. So let's get up super early on our last day. We will be arriving home around 10 tonight so let's set a wakeup call forrrr ohhh I don't know...the butt crack of dawn.

2. Mom is busy packing the suitcases so now is your chance to try on any outfits you like. Don't ever agree to the first one she chooses. That's why she brings extras. She wants to see you wear all of them. So peruse the suitcase at will. Don't bother to clean up after yourself. Mom lives for that crap.

3. Don't eat breakfast. It's a waste to eat the junk they already have in the hotel room. Wait until you leave the room for the day and ask for something obscure. Be adventurous and creative in your request.

4. If the bus to Downtown Disney is 45 minutes late wait until you see it rounding the corner before mentioning that you have to pee. Mom always did want to be a runner. No better time than the present.

5. Fight for your right to sit four rows away from your parents on the bus. It's a time to make new friends and they can't monitor you as well from a distance. This works if you have a sibling who likes to choose her own seat as well...four rows up from yours. Divide and conquer friends.

6. Do NOT under any circumstance get into that stroller willingly. It is a 100 lb. restrictive torture device that your father lugs around for his own pleasure. Rage against it.

7. Eat only 4 bites of rice at lunch. The parents have carbolicious snacks in the bag for the plane that are way better than "lunch". They keep the best stuff in there to appease you on the flight. Hold out for it.

8. When it's time to head to the airport keep reminding them that you want to stay. A tantrum is warranted. It shows the degree of commitment and love you have for the vacation. Melting completely to the ground is the ultimate thank you for a good time.

9. Fun fact: airports are incredibly fun to run through. Lure parents into a false sense of security by sticking close during check in. Encourage them to check the

stroller. Once it's gone run. Be free. Everyone thinks its adorable. Especially security.

10. Voice your grievances while waiting to get through security or to board the aircraft. Anything that's on your mind. Get it out now. In line. Melt into the floor in a fabulously theatrical performance. Scream "let go! You're not my parents!" when Dad attempts to carry you onto the gangway.

11. Once on board establish your space. Don't tolerate younger siblings and their baloney. Don't share your toys. Don't allow them to touch you or your things. Alert parents if this is a problem. Loudly and with gusto. Remember yesterday when you encouraged your sister to play on the metal bars at the Speedway ride and she fell and busted her face open? Now is a good time to open that wound back up. Literally.

12. Order apple juice to drink. When the stewardess brings you an amber beverage stiff arm it. She clearly has no clue that apple juice is orange. She is an idiot and should be fired. Kick the seat in front of you until she corrects her mistake.

13. Drink as much as you can so you can check out those awesome airplane bathrooms. It's like peeing in a closet. Bucket list material.

14. Ask mom if she farted. Many times. Claim she did. Loudly.

15. High five siblings for any extra fun behavior. Dumping an entire Dr. Pepper in mom's lap is high five and a fist bump. She gets to smell like Dr. Pepper but she doesn't need the calories. How grateful she shall be.

16. Approximately 3 minutes before landing send the signal to sibling to check out. Fall asleep on Dad and let sister fall asleep on mom. The juggling act that follows of parents attempting to gather belongings without waking us is priceless. The passengers and flight crew think it's hilarious and precious, and mom and dad turn into ninja acrobats. Win. Stay asleep juuuust until you get to the car. Then cry the whole way home because you're tired.

Bonus points if you pee the bed once at home.

To All the Workin' Girls I've Loved Before

This was my first column to ever win an award.

As I pulled away from my house on Southwest 21st Street for the last time, tears rolled down my cheeks. The corny country song on the radio played a small part, but it was more than that. I was closing a chapter in my life; one that started with tears on the same street.

When I drove into Gainesville four years ago, I was already counting the days until I moved away. My husband and I left our friends and our lives in Tallahassee to finish our college educations at UF. I was devastated. In my mind Gainesville could never live up to the good times and good people in Tallahassee that I was already aching to go back and visit.

We bought a tiny two-bedroom house in a not-so-great part of town, and we rolled into the neighborhood around one in the morning. After we parked the moving truck, we hopped in the car to grab something to eat.

We found a Subway still open across the street, and I settled for a meatball sub with ranch dressing and all the trimmings. As I skulked out of the store and plopped down in the passenger seat with my steaming foot-long I saw a woman (and I use the term loosely) leaning into the window of a pick-up parked next to my car.

The tall, dark and handsome lady was wearing a bright pink tube top, a blue wig and the tiniest black spandex shorts that had no business even existing. She, or he, glanced over his or her shoulder, gave my husband a wink and a smile and then returned to her business proposition.

I didn't have to say anything. I just looked at my husband in dismay and we drove away. It was the perfect display of what my life was sure to be like in stinky ol' Gainesville. Nothing but transvestite hookers and a steaming pile of...meatballs.

But as time went on, and the ladies of the evening disappeared from my neighborhood, I found myself reluctantly growing attached to Gainesville. That tiny two-bedroom house turned into a huge vault that housed the precious memories of my first few years of marriage. I found a new home at Tower Publications, where my passion for writing was ignited and appreciated. I even found myself hooked on meatball sub lunch dates with some of the best friends I've ever had.

Before I knew it, three years had come and gone, and I knew my time in Gainesville was coming to an end. My husband got an incredible job offer in Indiana that we couldn't turn down. And I found it strange that in just a short time I had gone from counting down the days with gleeful anticipation to counting down with saddened hesitation. I wasn't ready to close this chapter just yet. It was just too soon. And anyway, what could there possibly be in stinky ol' Indiana for me anyway?

But just like all good things, my time in Gainesville did come to an end. And as the last of the boxes were loaded into the trunk, the tears began to flow. I pulled out of my driveway for the last time, remembering the slip n' slide Fourth of July bashes and listening to the thunderstorms roll in from my screened porch. That thunder seemed to resonate in the pit of my stomach. I just wasn't ready to go.

But as I turned the corner and my house was just a dot in my rearview, I saw the Subway through my tears. And out in front, like a sign from above, was a tall, dark and handsome beauty with a bright pink tube top and the shortest shorts I'd ever seen. I slowed down a little in disbelief, and as I passed she, or he, gave me a wink and a smile.

I still miss my life in Gainesville. The people I left behind are some of the most precious gifts I've ever been given. But just as that working girl never left that

Subway, I know those memories will never leave my heart.

The Joys of Pregnancy

Ahh, the joys of pregnancy. The radiant glow, the elation of bringing life into the world and the excuse to eat as much as you want. It all looks so magical and wonderful – on paper.

The problem for me is that the radiant glow is usually just me sweating since I am now a human oven, the thought of being responsible for a human is sometimes terrifying, and for the first three months my relationship with food was touch and go. My stomach would touch it, and then it would go. Yes, I have discovered the joys of pregnancy are not always so joyful.

The real bummer of it all is that for the first three months, like most women, I didn't even look pregnant, so people just had to wonder if I had a drinking problem. I was walking around half asleep because I had to use the bathroom 14 times a night. I was constantly tossing my cookies in the nearest trash can, and my belly looked bloated as if I just hit the keg a little too hard. Basically I spent my first trimester trying to convince people I wasn't rushing a fraternity.

And according to the rules of society, it's my preggy duty to keep it to myself that I'd turned into a human factory. I couldn't just blurt out that my new physique and demeanor could be credited to the fact that I was busy making a complex nervous system and a four-chambered heart for a fellow human being.

No, no. Women are encouraged to wait until they are three months along before they share the joyous news.

In fact, it really isn't until you pass that three month mark that the doctors even treat your pregnancy like it's legit. Most get their nurses to deal with you until you get over that first trimester hump. It's kind of like "Well we did get the pregnancy test results back, but we're waiting to see if it takes." Like it's a flu shot. Delightful.

And I've gotten all sorts of helpful advice from women who have either forgotten what it was like to be pregnant or who are freaks of nature and not at all human. My mother-in-law likes to remind me that she never suffered a day of morning sickness. Oh and by the way, her child slept through the night at two days old.

I call shenanigans. I think these crazy women just forget the agony that is pregnancy. I've had plenty of women tell me to forgo the pain killers because "women are built for bearing children." Are you kidding? A rubber band is built to stretch around a newspaper, but sometimes they snap. And is there any recovering from that? I think not.

Now it probably does not help that I also got a surge of hormones strong enough to make me cry at shampoo commercials. But now I'm in my second trimester, which everyone keeps referring to as the honeymoon phase of pregnancy. And I have to admit it's nice to be able to brush my teeth once again without losing six ounces of stomach acid in the process. But what kind of honeymoon is this where I feel like maiming my husband because the water in the shower was too cold?

Lately I find myself lashing out at people like a crazed loon. And as I'm raving there is actually a voice in my head that says "You've lost it lady." But I can't stop. Like I told my poor husband, I think my give-a-damn's busted.

What kind of monster has pregnancy turned me in to? And why would anyone do this to themselves? I mean I actually did this on purpose. There was charting and testing and scientific calculations that went into achieving my knocked-up status. But why? Why would I wish this upon even my worst enemy?

Because of yesterday. Yesterday I felt it. The slightest most beautiful flutter I've ever felt. I was eating cherry fruit snacks when all of a sudden it felt like someone did a little tumbling routine in my tummy. It was so subtle, and yet in that instance I got the mommy amnesia. I forgot about all the gross, unpleasant and uncomfortable aspects of the pregnancy. All I could think about in that moment was the beautifully precious life I was helping to bring into the world. And at least for that moment I truly felt myself glow.

Fat is in the Eye of the Beholder

I got some startling news a few weeks ago from people whose opinions I hold in the highest regard. It rattles me to the core even to write it now, but it came from some reliable sources, so it must be true. My husband's gotten fat.

Now this came as an utter shock to me. As far as I knew he was just as hunky and ripped as the day I met him. I noticed that I've packed on the pounds since we've met. But I guess being the chubby chaser he is; he doesn't mind one bit.

He seems to be just as attracted to me, if not more, as the day we met. Even as everything including my waistband and I think a set of keys is devoured by my stomach, he still just can't help himself. He thinks I'm one hot mama.

And I really didn't understand it until recently. I always thought he was just being nice and pretending to find me irresistible, because seeing as he married me and all – I'm the only real shot at lovin' he's got. He always just seemed to view my physique through rose-colored beer goggles.

But a few weeks ago I finally realized I have a pair of goggles of my own. It was his dad's wife who first brought it to my attention that my husband's former firm form had morphed in to something a little cushier. She was harping on the fact that as his wife it was my duty to properly nourish him. She took my goggles off for a second and I saw that his cheeks did look a little chubbier. But no matter, my goggles were right back on within seconds and I pushed the thought aside.

Then my grandparents came for a visit and my Nana chimed in. Now my Nana is a very Southern woman with a sweet Texas drawl. Anytime you visit her house she is ready to feed you in a heartbeat. After helping yourself to two plates of food she'll say, "Well you hardly touched a thing. I guess you didn't like it." So as you're forcing down that third helping she'll reply "Why Crissy, you sure have put on a little weight."

So when she commented on Cary's little tummy he'd acquired I first chalked it up to the usual spiel. But then she started talking about me watching for signs of diabetes, of which apparently there are many. Things such as "using the potty too much" or eating three boxes of chocolate at a time put you at risk for the disease.

And for a split second she took my goggles off as well. I briefly saw that my hunky husband had morphed a little more into a chubby hubby. Why I declare, his tummy has a little more pooch than I'd remembered.

Now just a few years ago we both had put on some weight, and I heard about it from everyone and their brother. But while I fielded questions like, "Why are you fat now," from my grandfather, the husband was hearing, "You know Cary, you look good with a little extra weight on you."

Okay, so I'm no Olive Oyl, but he was no Popeye either.

So I have to admit that the comments in the past few weeks about his poundage were pretty refreshing to hear. Especially when accompanied by the few "And you look like you've lost weight," comments thrown my way. But the real head-scratcher was that due to the goggles, I really and honestly didn't notice his weight gain.

And then it came to me. I think we got those rose-colored beer goggles as a wedding gift. I don't quite recall who gave them to us, probably my crazy Aunt Phyllis. But I'm pretty sure that's the day that we etched the image of one another in our minds and hearts forever.

I still see him as that handsome young guy I marched down the aisle toward. All I could see was that cute little dimple that he only gets when he smiles a certain way. I saw his beautiful eyes sparkling because of the joyful tears welling up. And I guess I'll just always see him that way.

I think it's a gift that some lucky couples get. Those rose-colored beer goggles that let you see that person in the best light possible.

My grandparents had the same goggles. I remember my grandpa telling us that if the front door was locked, we'd better not knock. He loved all 75 pounds of my grandma until the day she left this earth. And I'm sure when he thinks of her now, it's still through those goggles.

Fighting the Fever

It's that time of year again when the cold weather and indoor confinement team up with lower immune systems to spread holiday crud. And there seems to be a serious fever spreading through so many women near and dear to my heart. Yes, I'm afraid that baby fever has taken hold of those poor souls, and thoughts of procreation are creeping into their heads.

Fortunately the runny noses and headaches that accompany this condition have been reason enough for me to avoid this nonsense like the plague. But my friends have not been so lucky. Several of them have already fallen pregnant, and even more are talking about getting some buns in those ovens.

Now the last time I had this fever I got it bad. I caught it from a little rascal named Cohen who was only one day old. I knew I should have worn some sort of gloves or something the first time I held him, but we were in a very sanitary hospital and he looked clean enough, so I thought what the heck. Well shame on me because that little booger gave me the worst case of baby fever I've ever known.

Oh it was horrible. Every time I passed a stroller I would get a stomach ache. Well I suppose it was more like butterflies, but oh I would moan and groan. Yes, it sounded more like oohs and aahs, but I definitely felt a strange chest pain. It was an aching in my heart for a tiny piece that was missing.

And once you catch the fever you are very susceptible to pregnancy. I think the statistics are something like 3 out of 4 women who catch baby fever end up pregnant within the next year. There should be some kind of awareness campaign. Maybe we should wear little ribbons to let people know how serious this is.

Naturally just a few months later I turned up preggers with twins. Now unfortunately that first pregnancy just didn't take, and it left me completely heartbroken. But oddly enough, it is a medical fact that a failed pregnancy was no match for the strain of baby fever I'd caught. So it was back to work. This fever of mine had me spending a lot of time in bed, not so much resting, but rather trying to create a tiny human.

Then, on what would have been my due date with the twins, I found out I was pregnant again. Now this one stuck like glue. And there has never been a more wanted or planned-for child in the history of the world. Despite the morning sickness, backaches, mysterious rashes and other delights that came with the manufacturing of a baby, I absolutely adored being pregnant. I instantly bonded with my precious daughter in utero. I talked to her and read to her, and once she was born it was all I could do to put her down long enough to catch a quick shower. I am completely and absolutely smitten with the child. However.

When she was 16 months I had some blood work drawn and a few labs run, and it turns out my baby fever has gone into remission. I, unlike these crazies surrounding me, have absolutely no desire to have another baby anytime soon.

As much as I love this darling angel of mine, how can I put this delicately? She ain't exactly the type that has yeh itchin' fer more.

She is so fun and inquisitive and brilliant and beautiful and funny, but good Lord help me if I had another just like her. I just lack the stamina. And these lunatic women who are either purposefully pregnant or looking to get that way are not first-timers. They are veteran moms who already have at least one child. How is it possible that they are considering having another when it's all I can do to keep up with the one I've got?

I sometimes think maybe there's something wrong with me. Maybe I'm just not woman enough for two kids. I mean the notion of more than one child is not a new one. I would say more often than not people opt for round two and sometimes round three and four. But by golly, some days I'm in the corner begging for mercy as it is. I am just not ready to say "Please sir may I have another?"

But I don't think that's it. I doubt I'm lacking any magic mothering skills that prevent me from having two kids. It all actuality I think I'm a little afraid to have another one because I'm having such a blast with this one. Right now it's just crazy fun, but if I added another one it would be complete chaos. I'll never get this one-on-one time back, and I really cherish it. Round two can wait.

As for those currently suffering from the fever who have perfect little first drafts, tee hee and good luck. If you get one like mine your second time out of the gate I have a feeling you'll get your immunizations next year.

This Ain't My First Rodeo

Ahh kids. I don't know how it happened but all of a sudden I'm just weeks away from delivering the second person I ever made. It seems like just yesterday I was trying so hard to make that first one. Then boom. My baby is 2 and I somehow managed to make another one.

Funny how that first baby differs from the next. Everything was magical with that first pregnancy. I started happily swallowing giant bricks marketed as prenatal vitamins the second we decided to think about possibly conceiving our first daughter. I silently, and sometimes not so silently, judged those horrible mothers who would even be in the same room as caffeine while they were pregnant. I made healthy food choices like carrot sticks and low fat yogurt, and I made it a point to walk around our neighborhood every evening while holding hands with my loving husband.

Bless this second child's heart. This entire pregnancy has been plagued by Beef n' Cheddar cravings and shameful bouts of Cheeto Puffery. And let's face it this child is no stranger to a Dr. Pepper. But give me a break, I've got to keep my energy up if I want to try and wrangle that escaped mental patient disguised as my 2-year-old. Between the 15 horsey rides and 10 tea parties each day, I really should be allotted more than the 200 milligrams of caffeine they allow. And I know that tea has to be decaf because I am more exhausted after the tea party than when we started. It's not just Earl Gray and crumpets. Rapunzel Barbie, one-armed sock monkey and Carla the lizard can all vouch for me. The girl knows how to party.

By the end of the day I'm just glad I remembered to feed myself as well as my child, and if we both have on real pants then it's a good day. Who has time to remember if I took that prenatal vitamin this morning? Wait, I think I'm supposed to take them at night. That cuts down on the morning sickness. Nothing like having your head in the toilet and your 2-year-old rubbing your back whispering, "You ok Momma? You barfing?"

Yes while I used to sit in my chair with my feet up smiling sweetly at the little angel kicking ever so sweetly at my round glowing belly, I now just try and shield my bump from the not-so-gentle high fives and fist bumps that her sister throws her way.

Don't get me wrong, I still think all the tumbling and rolling around in there is pure magic. I just wish the magic happened during Sunny's nap time rather than once I fall into bed exhausted at the end of the day. I'm assuming this contributes to the pregnancy insomnia I've developed.

If it's not one of the 30 bathroom trips I need in a night, or waking up to do a proper three-point-turn in order to face the other way in bed, it's my toddler hollering at me for a drink of water or to find some random stuffed animal we haven't seen in months that she absolutely 100 percent needs in order to sleep at that very moment. Once I tend to all those needs, if my husband's oh-so-soothing snoring doesn't prevent me from falling asleep, my little bun in the oven decides to make her presence known with a few double axles and a triple Sal chow just to show off.

It's not uncommon for me to wake up at 3 a.m. for the day simply because I can't fall back asleep. My super-observant spouse has questioned this nonsense several times. "You know," he said one night as I lay there reading quietly. "It's not healthy for you and the baby to stay up all night like that."

I wholeheartedly agreed with him, but tried to explain that I just couldn't sleep. He advised me just to turn off the Kindle and close my eyes for the good of the pregnancy. I told him I would.

My love rolled back over and settled into slumber in a matter of seconds. Immediately I started poking him repeatedly in the back. "What?" he asked in a slightly annoyed tone. "Nothing," I replied. "Just go to sleep."

He settled back in once again, and when I could tell he was out I started the nudging again. "What are you doing?" he asked, a little more grizzled. "Nothing," I replied. "Just go to sleep. It's not healthy for you to stay up all night." He rolled over and when he was almost asleep I started poking again and added, "But it sure as hell isn't easy to sleep with someone poking you awake either is it? Now pretend your back is your uterus. Goodnight."

Ahh the joys of pregnancy.

Can I See Some ID?

Last year I had to show two forms of identification, a bill in my name and pass a written exam to get my Indiana driver's license. I once had to pass a background check and a character assessment to adopt a mixed-breed terrier. And yet in a few short weeks I am going to be handed a brand spankin' new human to take home with no questions asked.

I consider myself a fairly well-adjusted member of society. I go to work every day, and I never call in sick unless I can't get out of bed. I haven't had a speeding ticket since I was 16, and I always wear my seatbelt in the car. I pay my bills on time each month, never carry a balance on my credit card and put a little away in savings for a rainy day. However, none of it matters to the fine medical staff who will soon hand me this fragile little creature. No, they pretty much hand these suckers over to anyone willing to birth them.

Now I did hear that they check to make sure you have a car seat for the wee one, and that it is properly installed. But they don't follow you home to make sure you don't just throw the kid down on a chair with your jacket while you go grab a sandwich. And these people do not come with manuals or any kind of instructions. It's just pop 'em out, clean 'em off and send 'em home. Just another day at the office for Dr. Huey and his staff.

Oh sure, we have friends who have children who we have played with and babysat for a few hours. They all survived. We have all the books about "What to Expect," and we go to child birthing and rearing class faithfully every Monday night. But we have never been in charge of another person full time before. My husband and I have hardly been in charge of ourselves for very long. How could we possibly be qualified to take home a brand new person?

But I think Mother Nature realized what silly creatures we humans are, and so she designed a crash course in parenting. We call it pregnancy.

I don't know how it was decided that humans need nine months to learn to care for an infant, but the parenting lessons learned during that time are priceless. And it is more than just Mom learning her new role. There are plenty of lessons for Dad too.

Lesson one comes about in the very early stages of the first trimester. For those men and women who wonder if they could handle a little spit up on their collar, Mother Nature sends in a delightful preview in the form of morning sickness.

Mom gets to spend her mornings, or afternoons, or evenings, or all of the above paying homage to the porcelain gods. And my husband got to benefit from the lesson as well since I was sick the entire 23-hour drive to see my family at Christmas. Trash bag after trash bag was filled with the fragrant aroma of Mexican food and stomach acid. While I had my head in the bag, he had his head out the window trying not to join me in my hurl fest. But we made it through, and on to lesson two.

'Round about the time my morning sickness started to subside, it was time to move on to our next parenting lesson. One of the common complaints of new parents is the endless crying that infants do day and night.

Well right there to welcome me into my second trimester were my raging hormones, and with them came the endless crying. I would keep my husband up night after night crying because I wasn't sure that he was going to properly bond with the baby. Or we had run out of milk for my cereal. The non-stop rollercoaster of emotion was enough to drive anyone to drink. But we got through it, and he learned to just talk to my belly and keep more milk in the house.

Lesson three is one that has gradually cropped up and supposedly just gets worse as I get closer to delivery. I think it is the one that is supposed to fog your mind enough so that you aren't rational enough to realize what an incredibly drastic change you are about to make in your life. It is the progressive sleep deprivation that arrives when you're in the home stretch.

Imagine swallowing a 10-pound feral cat whole and allowing it to live in your abdomen. Sometimes I swear the child is trying to break one of my ribs off to use as a pick axe to tunnel her way out of my womb. I have not been able to sleep on my back in 5 months, sleeping on my back will potentially kill my child, and now even rolling over in bed is an Olympic sport.

And if all the tossing, turning and grunting I do fails to wake my dear husband, then I find myself shaking him and asking for a push. Once I get rolled over and back to sleep, I usually have about 20 minutes before I am up again to go to the bathroom. And from what I have been told, the restless nights continue until the baby is born when they turn from restless to sleepless. Oh joy.

However, I have realized that without these parenting lessons we glean during pregnancy, it would be too overwhelming to be given this delicate little creature. At least having conquered these preliminary lessons, we are better prepared to tackle the nitty gritty tiring job of being a parent.

And I know that I still have so much to learn, but at least now when they hand over my baby girl I can feel a little more qualified than I was nine months ago. And hey, if those pregnancy lessons didn't make me feel like I earned that little bundle of joy, then I'm sure it's nothing a good 24 hours of blood, sweat and tears in labor and delivery couldn't help with.

The Karma of Miss Frizz

I think we all had that one substitute teacher in school who we just knew was a total whack-job. Maybe they smelled funny, or they told the same lame story to every class they subbed in. My weirdo was Ms. Kirkland, my ninth grade French class permanent, or not-so-permanent, sub.

Ms. Kirkland walked into my French class with her frizzy red hair and smeared red lipstick looking like a severely disheveled Miss Frizzle from the Magic School Bus books.

She wore out-dated clothes like stirrup pants and shoulder-padded shirts. But she always had a smile on her face and a kind, but crazy voice.

The poor woman might have survived a third grade science class, but she didn't stand a chance with these too-cool-for-school ninth-graders. The first day Ms. Kirkland, or as I came to know her Miss Frizz, arrived we took it easy on her. She only got spit wads on her back and the simultaneous 9 a.m. coughing fit from the class. Her lip only quivered slightly as she tried to keep her crazy voice stable that day. But she made it.

I'm not sure why we were so heinous. I guess it was to delay learning to say "J'aime le fromage." But by the end of the week, all bets were off and the class was ready to be rid of Miss Frizz.

After sending her stalking through the class trying to figure out where that mysterious hum was coming from, two boys somehow managed to lock her in the closet for rest of the period. Needless to say that was the last time I ever saw Miss Frizz.

Now, of course I was not involved in this torture directly. But I also did nothing to stop it. And that is how I found out about the karma of Miss Frizz.

December 2006 I graduated with my journalism degree and decided that maybe I had a calling to teach. And so I thought I would take a semester to substitute teach to get my feet wet.

My first day on the job was a first grade class, which I thought would be full of finger paints and hugs. Eight exhausting hours later, I collapsed on the couch and didn't move for the rest of the night. Those first graders aren't so cute when they're running around the room screaming for an hour or trying to flush an entire roll of toilet paper, cardboard and all. But if that was my worst day on the job, I would have been lucky.

The next day I received a big dose of karma for my idle amusement at Miss Frizz's expense.

I was filling in for a 10th grade English teacher, which was more than perfect since that was exactly the what I wanted to teach.

I was all too proud of myself when first period went smoothly and my desires to teach the youth of America were confirmed. I even called my mom during my planning period to tell her how wonderful teaching was.

And then third period happened.

I should have gone home three minutes in when the class wadded up their quizzes and threw them at me. But I was still jazzed from first period.

Then one sweet boy repeatedly refused to clear his desk during the quiz, so I decided to make an example of one thinking the rest would follow.

I picked the wrong kid.

I took his iPod and sweater off the desk and told him he could get them after class. As I turned my back to put them on the desk the six-foot-tall kiddo got up and slammed me up against the desk cursing and yelling at me to give him his things back. I was completely caught off guard. I just assumed the plastic id badge and heels would give me immunity.

As I saw none of the students were going to rescue me, I touched two fingers to each of his elbows, looked him in the eyes and told him to back away. He threw my hands away and started shrieking that I hit him. He grabbed his things and flew out the door.

The class was silent, and I didn't follow him. Instead I just got through the day, and waited until I got in my car to start wailing to my husband about what had happened.

I was scared, and I couldn't believe that no one came to my rescue. But more so I felt like I had failed as a teacher.

After a few months of death threats and smart mouths I realized that my desire to educate had faded like acid-washed jeans. I turned back to journalism where the most dangerous thing I'd encountered was the occasional reptile or approaching deadline. But I gained a new respect for the educators in my life, and felt remorse for some I'd encountered.

So as this new school year begins, I would like to take a moment to say thank you to those teachers who inspired me and apologize to those I gave grief. I've walked half a mile in your shoes and believe me, my feet are killing me!

Home for the Holidays

Since I was a kid the holiday season has been my favorite time of the year. The heaps of presents and decadent food are all fine and well, but it's the predictability and tradition that I have come to love and rely on. November was always my security blanket that I could count on to be the beginning of the season of same old same old.

However now that I'm all grown up, married and have my new baby Sunny, my life is full of blissful chaos. It's now become a crapshoot as to where we'll be each holiday. My family lives in Texas, and my husband's family members are scattered in Florida and Louisiana. Since we moved to Indiana it is increasingly difficult to find the time and resources to see everyone during the holidays. This may be the first year that I don't go back "home" for the holidays.

When I was younger my holiday schedule was as consistent as French's French Fried Onions on a green bean casserole. Thanksgiving lunch was at Nana's followed by dinner at Grandma's. Nana would have turkey and noodles and Papaw's famous King Ranch casserole. After lunch we would draw names for Secret

Santa and try not to spill the beans about who we picked.

After Nana's I would head to Grandma's house where I somehow always managed to make room for more turkey and gravy. Grandma would make sure everyone took home their own loaf of pumpkin bread and Grandpa would have to make double the mashed potatoes just because of me.

Just as the tryptophan wore off and I could fit back into pants without an elastic band, Christmas would come barreling right around the corner. On Christmas Eve my brother, Tyler, and I would head over to Nana's house for dinner. The kids would squirm and fidget after dinner waiting for the green light to dive into the presents. Last year at 24 I was still squirming and fidgeting right along with them.

That night back at Mom's house we would exchange just one gift from each other. It was the best part of Christmas to see Mom open her gifts from us. She would ooh and ahh over a macaroni necklace with the same enthusiasm as a Waterford crystal vase--maybe even more so with the necklace.

After the exchange we would head to bed, and even though last year my husband and I were 24, and Tyler was 19; Mom would still wait until we were asleep to wrap and place our presents under the tree.

Around 4 on Christmas morning Tyler and I would tiptoe out of our room to sneak a peek at our presents. The room would be dark except for the glow of the Christmas tree, and I would still get worried about Mom catching us out of bed.

After we opened Santa's gifts we would head out to Grandma's for more presents, food and family time. We stayed until late into the night and played so many hands of cards that we had to use the toothpicks from the veggie trays to keep our eyelids open.

It was a time full of tradition and family that I knew I could count on. The stress from school, a fight with a friend, the loss of a job or a loved one could all be swept away for a short time during the holidays because it was a time just to focus on family and togetherness.

Nana's, Mom's, Grandma's; they were all safe places that housed the refreshing dose of love and laughter I needed once a year. Even after I left for college I knew I could rely on those traditions to be there waiting for me as if nothing had ever changed.

Of course as is life, things did gradually change. I got married and had to learn to split holidays with my husband's family, and Grandma passed away so Grandpa had to do the Christmas shopping alone. This year we have the baby, so driving 20 hours to Texas is out of the question. And flights are so outrageous it is questionable whether I'll get to see my family at all this holiday season.

I can see those traditions I have come to rely on slowly vanishing. It's hard to think about a Christmas without Papaw parading around in his goofy Santa hat or Grandpa letting me sneak the first taste of the turkey. It seems like my family traditions are slowly slipping away and it breaks my heart.

But on the other hand, I suppose the traditions aren't vanishing, they're only changing. Instead of King Ranch casserole at Nana's, I get to fix my famous cranberry bread for my father-in-law at my house. And instead of sneaking to peek at the tree with my baby brother, I get to see my baby girl open her first present on Christmas morning.

I guess the warm comfort of the holidays isn't about falling into the same routine year after year. It's about evolving with the changes life has in store, and it's making new memories and traditions with the people you love. After all, there had to be a first Thanksgiving at Nana's house. So rather than going home this holiday season to see my family, I will help make this my family's home for the holidays.

Mushy Love Stuff

There are those couples who broadcast their love via Facebook. They tag their significant other and talk about all the magical ways they're in love and end with something touching like "love my life." Then there are those couples you see at parties or restaurants that are just so wrapped up in each other they might as well be in a world all by themselves. Their eyes sparkle as they ask "Hey babe, will you pass the snoogie boogie?" And only their partner will giggle and know the secret code for pass the salt.

These kids just really seem to have it together, and I've caught myself a time or wishing and maybe even wondering aloud why my Hubs and I are the couple who are saying things like "Dude just pass the pepper and quit farting around." Our relationship just seemed to be lacking that spark everyone else had.

I knew a guy in high school who was totally in love with a girl I'll call Kelly. She was slightly out of his league and kept him in the friend zone pretty diligently. But he enlisted the help of about 20 girls in our class to woo her, and in the name of love we all agreed to do our best. Well perseverance paid off, and she agreed to go out on one date. He must have really put on his game face, because he won a second and then a third date. They went off to college together and in proper fairy tale form they got married. They adopted a beagle and were living a fabulous life in the big city just head over heels in love.

The Hubs and I met up with them a few years ago at a wedding, and I couldn't help but be a little envious of how in love this guy still was with his high school sweetheart. Don't get me wrong, Hubs and I love each other, but he just didn't look at me with those googley eyes any more.

Our firstborn was just a year old at the time, so we spent the whole time trading off chasing her around. And when all the other couples were out on the dance floor, we sat it out and he worked recon while I tried to discreetly breastfeed our active little monkey in the middle of a ritzy wedding reception.

For years I thought about that couple as the epitome of love. They were just one of those pairs that were destined for each other and would be old and grey in the rocking chairs holding hands and more in love than ever. I strived for it, and I tried to force that kind of smooshy gushy stuff into my marriage, but to no avail. With kids and work and keeping up the house and life we were just a well-oiled machine. But we rarely had any mush.

Friday I got sick. I mean really sick. To top it off our 3-year-old started vomiting for 24 hours straight, and the baby couldn't stop coughing long enough to eat. Even if she could, my milk was so hot from my fever that she didn't want to nurse. I just laid there in bed with kids screaming and climbing all over me wallowing in misery. That's when the Hubs texted to check in on me. He's been doing that since we got married. He calls or texts in the morning to see how my day is going, and on this particular morning I just grumbled and told him about the joys I was experiencing.

Twenty minutes later the door opens and in walks the Hubs with Sprite, pain relievers and all the makings for chicken and dumplings. Without saying a word he kissed my forehead, took the kids into the living room, started boiling the chicken, cleaning the kitchen and fixing me some Sprite and a cup of tea.

I spent the rest of the day in bed recovering and reflecting a bit on what it really means to love someone. I opened up my Facebook to broadcast to the world what a great Hubs I have, when something caught my eye.

Kelly's status was changed from married to single. I just about fell out of bed. After sifting through some posts from her mother and emailing a few trusted sources, I discovered that Kelly's beau, the one who worked like crazy for one date and treated her like the jolly Queen of England, had been having an affair with a co-worker for years.

I decided to go with a lighter Facebook status post about the Hubs cleaning up vomit rather than getting all gushy and flowery about what a fabulously adorable and caring husband I have. But if you read between the lines you can see we are one of those blissfully happy couples. Our mush is just made of something a little stronger.

Trailer Park Treasure

The good news was that Hubs got the job he'd been seeking since we were just a couple of young Gator grads. We'd be moving closer to family and raise our babies back in the South. Back to Texas. Back home. The bad news was that his start date was in six weeks and Christmas was in five days.

With less than a week before we started our annual family holiday trek around the country, we had to de-clutter our house, get it on the market, pack our bags for our two-week holiday travels, oh yeah – and find a new place to live. I stayed up every night until at least 2 a.m. shoveling crap we never used into boxes I secretly hoped I'd never see again. And as we sat in our nearly bare living room we pondered over where to stash our family until we could sell our old house and find something new.

We kicked around the idea of an apartment, but we didn't like the thought of having to move all our crap into one place just to have to then move it out again. And the rent for a decent apartment was more than our mortgage payment. Even if we happened to find a new house, we couldn't close on it in only six weeks, especially since it might be a while before we sold our old one.

Then Hubs had a little light bulb flicker. We would stay in our camper. Why not? We loved going camping, and it would only be temporary. Two adults, a 3-year-old and an infant shacked up in 150 square feet of fiberglass glory. What could possibly go wrong? The rent on the campsite was pennies compared to an apartment, plus you got 20 channels of free cable. Win.

So on a dreary day in February we tearfully said goodbye to our dear 2,200 square foot sanctuary and set off towing The Wilderness.

When we ran this master plan by friends and family we heard things like "Oh my God why," and "You'll end up divorced."

So we were extra excited to get set up with so many people confident we'd succeed. But we survived the first night. We all took turns bathing 20 minutes apart in the shoe box of a shower, including my mother who helped drive us down. You needed to wait at least 20 minutes so you'd have three minutes of hot water stored up. And as I lay in the luxurious queen sized fold-a-bed with the baby, Hubs snuggled up on the couch bed with our toddler's foot in his face and a super comfy metal bar in his back. We had arrived.

With each passing day I expected to yearn for square footage. I thought I'd desperately miss all the comforts of home like a dishwasher or an in-house washer and dryer. But a week passed and I was hanging in there just fine.

There wasn't room in the camper for too many toys, so the girls just had a small box with about six things that they treasured more than life itself. I saw my toddler invent stories with a pink stuffed owl and a naked Barbie doll that could win a daytime Emmy. Dinner was easy because it had to be. I didn't have a big prep area, so we survived off my Nana's tried and true recipes like macaroni and tomatoes or sausage and potatoes. And I couldn't stock the fridge, so a lot of nights dinner was take out. I certainly didn't miss a dishwasher on those nights.

We started traditions of donuts on Saturday mornings and tamale Tuesdays. With only 20 cable stations, seven of which were in Spanish, the entertainment pickings were slim. So we found ourselves playing Yahtzee and going for family walks after dinner.

The campsite office staff knew the girls by name and liked to treat my toddler to an ice cream bar when we came to get change for the laundromat. And the people watching I experienced while folding my skivvies in public was top notch.

But eventually we stumbled upon our dream home. It had all the features we were looking for, a beautiful view of the rolling hill country, and almost double the square footage of our old house. But as I packed up those six little toys and did one last 5 minute clean of my entire residence, I was a little sad to end our trailer park saga.

The months we spent in that little camper were some of the simplest and happiest memories our family has ever had. We didn't have things to distract us from one another. And we didn't have square footage to separate us. Being closer brought us closer, and I will forever be grateful that we had the privilege to live in our little trailer park home.

Home is Where the Crumbs Are

Since we were in college my husband and I knew we wanted to live in the South, but all his prospective jobs led us to the great white north. I sucked it up pretty good when we moved to Indiana. Ok I went kicking and screaming and vowed never to love anything or anyone that side of the Mason-Dixon Line. After all how could a place so far away from everything and everyone I knew and loved ever feel like home?

The year I moved to Gainesville from Tallahassee I made a similar vow. I could never learn to love Gator Country after being so happy in the land of the Seminoles. But four years after I moved in with tears in my eyes, I moved away with them streaming down my face. And now four years after we moved to Indiana, we got the job offer that will lead us back down south. Back home.

The Hubs has applied at this company plenty of times before, but never got a bite. I was ready to write them off this time too until the offer came through.

I've imagined that moment for four years. I thought I'd shriek with joy, call my mom, text my friends and alert the presses that we were finally going home. But when the moment came, my husband and I rationally talked out the logistics and I looked around at the catastrophe that was my house. The new company wanted us there in just a few weeks so we had to get the house on the market, I had two kids with pneumonia and I needed to pack for us to be gone for two weeks. And I had five days to get it all done. I started to panic a little as I watched Sunny leave a trail of cracker crumbs down the hall.

The next day I flew into packing mode. I started boxing everything up that we wouldn't need to try and clear the clutter and get the house "show ready." I was supposed to be excited and ready to get back to the warm sunshine of the south, but with each box a little piece of my heart was broken.

As I packed Sunny's room I couldn't figure out where I was going to keep all the artwork she made in preschool. The same preschool where she gets to see all her friends, and the one she begs to go to when we're on vacation or summer break. I remember being so nervous as I dropped her off on the very first day at that school, and then watching my little girl march into Miss Gayle's class like she owned the joint.

I decided to take a break from packing and flopped down in a chair in the hearth room. The same chair I labored in when I was pregnant with Violet. The same chair she would have been born in if the Hubs hadn't casually suggested we might want to get to the hospital. The same chair that was her favorite to nurse in on those long sleepless newborn nights. The creak of the floorboard under that chair put her to sleep every time like a trusty lullaby.

But there was no time for sentiment; it was time to get this house ready for market. When the realtor came to assess it, she brought comps and talked numbers, but when it came to putting a price on our house I just didn't know how. She talked square footage and bonus space, but this place is full of memories that are stitches in the fabric of our family.

When we moved from our house in Gainesville it was just Cary and me. It was our first house as a married couple, so I thought it would be the most special house we ever left. But now as this house is being emptied of our worldly possessions it's easier to see the ghosts of the life we've built here. This was our first house as a family. Our children were born here, we had our first Christmas as a complete foursome, my little dog Cuddles is buried in the backyard, and we've made true friends we'll cherish our whole lives long.

So as we leave here, I make a new vow. I will leave my heart open to our new home in the South. I will not vow against loving it nor will I swear against making new friends. But I know now that each new place our life takes us, we will leave a little trail of crumbs from our hearts.

Don't Be Such a Wiener

Giving birth to my second daughter was the most invigorating and wonderful experience of my entire life. I'm also one of those ridiculous women who think pregnancy is a beautiful time full of rainbows and unicorns. The first three trimesters are filled with little magical wonders that I cherish and love.

But that fourth trimester, you know, the one where you actually get to hold and cuddle that little miracle you created inside your body? Well that one is for the birds my friend. I never want to do that nonsense again in my life. The cocktail of post pregger hormones and sleep deprivation trumps morning sickness, backaches and cankles any day. I'd gladly let someone put their baby inside me. But by God when that little darling is born it can go keep someone else awake at night.

Now the Hubs and I rarely agree. It's what keeps things spicy around here. But one thing we can come together on is the idea that we are only marginally equipped to handle two offspring. An even number just makes it easier for dinner reservations and Disney rides. So that settles it. We will become a two-kid household. We have opted to play a man to man defense instead of a zone. So the only decision to make was who should pull the proverbial plug on our procreation.

Now let it be known that this was not a long conversation, we were both stone cold sober, and we were both fully clothed. We might have actually been at Denny's at the time, so rest assured I could not use my womanly temptations to sway this verdict.

But my manly man husband offered to sacrifice his own vas deferens in the interest of our family of four fantasy. Was it because he witnessed me stoically giving birth to his child without so much as a Tylenol? Or is it the idea of screwing with my hormones, which aren't the most reliable on a good day anyway? We may never know. But he gets 150 cool points and a gold star for offering to go under the knife, or tiny little scopey thingy, whatever they use to do all that.

And since I did birth a child, and he had to have an emergency appendectomy this year anyway, we were at our deductible and just looking for procedures to get done this calendar year. So one Friday afternoon he chugged a beer, marched into the doctor's office, and just half an hour later walked bow legged into a weekend of frozen peas, extra strength ibuprofen and watching golf from his recliner.

I was pretty impressed with how quickly he healed from the whole thing. He milked it on Saturday, started fiddling around the house on Sunday, rode his motorcycle to work Monday and played two softball games Tuesday. The man really did bounce back good as new. Plus he got prescription conjugals. An added bonus of the procedure.

However, his father was less than thrilled at the thought that his boy had nixed any chances of having a son of his own. I'm pretty sure I was in trouble for not producing a male heir. Poor fella didn't get the memo that it's my hubby's boys that determine whether I'll have boys. But whatevs. I was charged with taking my husband's manhood on top of it.

He and others like him were completely appalled that my husband would agree, let alone offer, to give up his virility instead of me. I should have just tied my fallopians in pretty little bows and been happy to have to privilege. My father-in-law actually told my mother-in-law, "I hope you know there's no way in hell I'd ever do that."

I was worried my Hubs might feel pressure from all the negativity and brow beating these other "men" were giving him over this very personal and fairly heroic decision. After all I do literally have his tubes sitting in a little jar in the cabinet. But he didn't even flinch. Well not because of all the razzing. I'll bet he flinched at some point during the actual snippety snip.

But my baby's daddy is man enough to shut off the supply valve without fearing that the whole factory will go kaput. So we giggle at our buddies who are done having kids, but are too afraid of losing their manhood to take care of business. One pal tried to convince his wife's doctor to just go ahead and tie her up when she goes in for her cesarean.

So while they're all scared out of their mind of having a little oopsie baby and avoiding each other like the plague, my fella is getting all the action because we know we're in the clear. It's downright liberating. So to all those "men" out there demanding their wives undergo yet another traumatic construction project on their nether bits I say, "Your wife's been through enough you wieners. Grow a pair and get it done."

The Mother of All Father's Days

Since I was a kid Father's Day has been to me what Valentine's Day is to single people: just a bitter reminder of a void in my life. My dad passed away when I was 9 years old leaving me to spend every Father's Day loathing those lucky children who got to make macaroni ties and ugly coffee mugs. Sure I had my grandfathers to think of. I gave them an obligatory call and a card. Some years I even made them pasta pictures. But I always had to write "I love you Grandpa" or "I love you Papaw." I never got to write "I love you Dad." That third Sunday in June was always a sad one for me, and it was one I never expected to enjoy again.

I did get a little glimmer of hope back when I got married. I inherited a pretty rad father-in-law who absolutely adores me. Over the years we've become so close, and he's helped to fill that fatherly gap by treating me like the daughter he never had. With three sons and no daughters, I am quite the commodity. And that first year we were married I got to write "I love you Dad" in a Father's Day card for the first time in 11 years.

Since my husband has a severe allergy to greeting cards, the special occasion card and gift responsibilities fall completely to me. So when Father's Day rolls around, I'm out looking for just the right frame for a family picture or a cheesy tie that his dad will think is hilarious. And it's all for the better because I can appreciate the privilege of having someone to buy a silly tie for more than anyone.

Two years ago I went and bought the Mack Daddy of all Father's Day presents. I waddled my 10-month pregnant self to the store and got the manliest meat smoker I could find. I couldn't wait to present it to the coolest father-to-be I knew; my husband.

He was so stoked he went out and bought a pork butt to smoke that morning. We put the butt in the smoker, and he opened his first Father's Day card.

I told him how excited I was for him to be a father and how great I knew he would be. I even did the cheesiest thing I could think of and bought him a snazzy calculator watch he'd been eyeing and said it was "from the baby."

As he opened the dorkiest present ever bestowed upon a man, I thought I felt something odd. It felt a bit like my water had broken. Sure enough, I was in labor. Our daughter was all about timing, calculator watch present and all.

Twenty-two hours later I gave birth to our baby girl and brought a new father into my life as well. It was another sweet gift to remind me to smile on that special Sunday in June.

Well just a few weeks ago was my baby's second birthday party. Our family was here, including some of the special fathers in my life. Since her birthday falls so close to Father's Day, and the family was all here anyway, we celebrated Father's Day along the weekend of her birthday.

The next day I was completely exhausted from the extravaganza that masqueraded as a toddler's birthday party. I guess all the late nights of cleaning, cooking and decorating finally caught up with me. At one point, for no apparent reason, I got pretty snippy with my husband. And it escalated into a knock-down drag-out with the most important father in my life right in front of our entire family.

My father-in-law hated to see us fighting, and he told my husband to try to smooth things out. The last time he remembers us having a big fight like this was right before I found out I was pregnant with Sunny. We had her to think about now, so all this fussing had to stop.

That's when the light bulb came on. The last time I had such a bad mood swing was when I was…that's right folks. I took the test and it is official. I'm pregnant again. We were completely overjoyed and shocked.

And we just cracked up thinking about my ridiculous mood swings that apparently just crop up when I get preggers.

My husband couldn't believe I was actually pregnant. Since our daughter was born we haven't exactly been the wild and crazy bedmates we once were. Most nights a 9 o'clock bedtime is the sexiest thing I've ever heard of.

Then my husband declared that he knew the exact day we got pregnant. He knows of three days a year that he's guaranteed a VIP Pass to Conjugal Town. One day is his birthday, and that was months ago in March. The second is our anniversary, but that isn't until early August. But the other day that he knows he's entitled to some horizontal hokey pokey is none other than the most important day of the year, Father's Day.

Welcome to the Jungle

I think just about every married guy or gal has a moment or two of longing for those carefree single days they once knew. While our single friends are out sowing their wild oats, the only oats we get are served lukewarm and semi-crusted over in a bowl with raisins. The hum drum normalcy of day-to-day married life can seem a little mundane in comparison to the non-stop party our single friends seem to have. It's hard not to long for a wild night out.

I was recently working on a story about a guy's idea of a perfect date. All I had to do was ask 10 random men about their idea of a perfect night out with a lady. As usual my procrastination left me grasping at straws the night before my story was due. So, I called one of my husband's friends hoping he'd be up for a quick interview, and he agreed. I asked where I could meet him, and since it was St. Patrick's Day he was at a bar downtown.

After I got my toddler settled in to bed, I threw my hair up in a ponytail, wiped the chewed up pasta off my t-shirt, traded my pajama pants in for a pair of ripped but comfy jeans, and I headed to the bar alone for the first time in seven years.

Now the last time I was in a bar looking for guys I had no trouble finding plenty of gentlemen who were willing to give me attention. I'm not saying I was pick of the litter, but one of these fellas did marry me. Let's just say my milkshake brought a respectable crowd of boys to the yard.

But seven years later, here's a fun-fact: Just as the scent of a human will scare wild game away from the hunter, the stench of marriage and children will repel male bar patrons from a woman. You see the last time I went sauntering through a bar, I was a 19-year-old blonde-haired blue-eyed college co-ed. I dolled myself up with make-up, smelly good sprays and tight jeans. Back then the tight jeans said, "Come hither gentlemen." Now they just look like they're crying, "Help me! I'm being zipped against my will!"

The interview I got from my friend Dan was the only one willingly given that night. I spent the next five hours fighting my way through a jungle of testosterone. And I discovered two different species of guys inhabiting the bar scene that night.

The first were the Marrieds. Because this particular breed has been in captivity for so long, they were the most tame and easiest to approach. However, they were the least comfortable to talk to about dating because it is such a primitive concept they can hardly remember.

They're used to traveling in pairs, so they were often in the company of another human. That person was either their wife, or their single buddy. The men who were with their wives were willing to talk, and by that I mean their wives forced them to repeat exactly what they were told.

The perfect date ideas I got from this group were all eloquently delivered by their chaperoning spouse. The Marrieds who were savoring a few hours of freedom with their single pals were not as willing to give interviews. I was informed that they were afraid to be quoted without prior approval from their wives, and that they couldn't quite remember what a date was supposed to be. Isn't that a shriveled fruit that was supposed to "keep them regular?"

After only two successful interviews from the Marrieds, I moved on to the other species, the Singles. The Singles were the scarier of the two breeds. The Singles I encountered was on high alert for any female activity in the surrounding area. They were ravenous for female attention, but also cautious not to engage with any of the Marrieds or the dreaded Single Mothers that might be lurking in the bar. I approached these boys with caution because I realized my wedding ring was still sitting by the sink. Stupid dishes. I was stepping into the lion's den wearing meat cologne.

The stupid meat cologne threw them off the scent of my married/breeder status. And while I have to admit I was flattered when the first one offered to buy me a drink, I desperately wanted to get this story done and get back to my pajama pants.

I decided that my opening line should inform them that I was there on business. However, "Hi there, I'm working on a story about dating," was apparently the oldest pick-up line in the book. Some were desperate enough to ignore my breeder scent, but others took one look at my disheveled appearance and knew I had the start of a litter at home. One guy even told me "Look you're pretty enough to get my attention, but I don't know if it's enough to get the interview." Ouch.

It took me hours to find just seven guys who weren't either trying to get me in bed, or repulsed when they learned I was married with an offspring. At 1:30 a.m. I'd managed to find seven guys who were either desperate enough for female attention, decent enough to see that I was truly working on a story, or just drunk enough to give me an interview. It was exhausting.

That night, as I wearily snuggled up to my very own Married boy, I had a new appreciation for my boring ol' married status. And I have a new respect for my single girl friends who brave the dating world.

It is a jungle out there.

I Found Life Lying Face Down in the Water

Reports that Americans take less vacation than our European counterparts are nothing new. A quarter of Americans don't get any paid vacation at all, and those who do get on average 12 to 14 days. The majority of people surveyed admit to using the internet and smart phones while on vacation to keep in touch with the office. And workers must feel that two full weeks is much too generous because on average they leave two to six days unused at the end of each year. I almost threw up when I read that little morsel. I live for vacation.

When the Hubs and I were in premarital counseling convincing the pastor that we were legit, he asked us why we wanted to get married. Our answer was that we had fun together. It sounded juvenile I'm sure, but now almost ten years later I can honestly say the fun times are probably the main reason we've made it through all the rough patches.

The first time I realized how strong my feelings were for my future Hubs was on a trip to Orlando. We were in Disney staying at my mom's timeshare, and the first morning we were there I woke up at 7 a.m. ready to roll. A humdrum fact, until you realize that 7 a.m. didn't exist in my world. I only considered myself a morning person because I rarely went to bed before 2 a.m. In those days 9 a.m. was a stretch for a wake-up call, and I was pretty much the most miserable soul on earth until 10:30 a.m. But that morning I woke up at 7:00 with a smile on my face ready to hit the parks like a 5-year-old with a sugar high. Some women settle down with a man who can get them into bed. I chose one who could get me out.

From then on we lived to travel. At the very minimum we'd take the motorcycle on a day trip to the beach. Our funds were limited, but our sense of adventure was not. Seeing a three-day weekend on the calendar was euphoric. It didn't have to be an extravagant trip. Some of our most precious memories were spent in a tent in the middle of the Florida wilderness. But sitting at home just wasn't an option.

The first vacations we took as a married couple were in the days before smart phones, or at least in the days before we could afford smart phones. No matter where we went we were completely unplugged. With each mile we inched closer to our destination, and I could see the coils of my tightly wound OCD engineer husband start to slowly unwind until we arrived and he was a totally relaxed free man. The burdens of work and school had no choice but to stay home because we only had room for so much baggage in our tiny Chevy Aveo. And those bags were jam packed with swim suits and sunscreen. Sorry troubles, you'll be here when we get back.

We always talked about renewing our vows at 10 years as long as we still thought this whole marriage thing was a good idea. With only a year left until our decabration we've talked about where to hold the ceremony. We've mentioned Hawaii or Sandals; we always tend to gravitate to somewhere with coconuts. But I think the destination that makes the most sense is the tiny key of Bahia Honda.

Before we graduated from UF and the responsibilities of life and jobs and kids overtook us we took a camping trip each May to Bahia Honda. It was just us, a tent, a cooler full of beer and the crystal blue waters of this unspoiled little island off the tip of Florida. We couldn't get reception if we wanted to. And we never did.

We once spent an entire day sitting in about a foot of water. We had the sunshine, our snorkeling masks and no sense of time. There we were face down in the water marveling at this tiny slice of life that most people never see. Even avid beach goers would miss the tiny flounder no bigger than a pencil eraser, but we got to see all these incredible creatures because we took time to slow down.

To this day when things get crazy and hectic, we go back to that moment our eyes met in those clear blue waters. We saw a lot of things that afternoon, but it was what we didn't find on the ocean floor that brought the most joy. We didn't see a clock, or an email, or a text. There were no deadlines hiding in the sand, and the only thing that crashed were the gentle waves on the beach.

I won't ever look back on my life and wish I'd spent more time hunched over a desk, but I might regret not spending a few more days lying face down in the water.

The Sacred Calf

Growing up in Texas the cow was sacred. If it ain't brisket it ain't barbecue. Ground beef is its own food group, and cow tippin' is a great way to spend a Friday night. I grew up worshiping the cow, and now the cow has betrayed me.

I've always had a taste for beef, but while pregnant with my baby Sunny I craved another cow commodity. Dairy was my vice and I indulged at will. I ate a bowl of cereal every morning, a bowl of ice cream each night and smothered or stuffed all other edibles with cheese.

Milk is loaded with calcium and vitamin D right? So I figured the more the merrier. But when my little lady was born, she was plagued with eczema, congestion and gastrointestinal woes all caused by the cow's milk proteins in my breast milk. What it boiled down to was no more ice cream, no more cheese and constant vigilance and examination of every ingredient of every food item I even considered putting in my mouth.

At first I thought it would be no big deal. Just steer clear of cheese, ice cream and swap in the soy milk on my cereal. Little did I know that food manufacturers like to beef up their protein numbers by adding whey to everything. Bread, salt and vinegar chips, my favorite golden arched French fries all had hidden dairy. I Can't Believe It's Not Butter might as well be butter because it's made with milk products, and soy yogurt wasn't safe either. My life turned into a CSI investigation of food labels.

The first few months were like going through detox. I got headaches and craved cheese constantly. It was hard to be around people eating bacon cheeseburgers, and I think I cried a little when Cary ate the last ice cream sandwich in the freezer. The hardest part wasn't figuring out what I couldn't eat, it was finding things I could eat.

Initially I stuck to raw fruits and veggies and plain meat. I thought dairy was the only seasoning in the world. Then I met Katie.

The only place in Texas Katie wouldn't offend the cattle gods is Austin because let's face it, Katie is weird. Not only is she a total hippie, she is a vegan. The girl eats no animal products whatsoever. But her daughter was the same age as Sunny and our love of crafting and lack of housekeeping skills drew us together.

We started hanging out a lot so the girls could play. We started sewing together, and eventually I spent quite a few afternoons at her house around lunch time. Since she didn't do the dairy dance either, the logistics were perfect for Sunny and me. But logistics are one thing and taste is another. I couldn't think of anything without meat or cheese that would sound tasty. But boy was I wrong.

I feasted on a mouthwatering mixed grill of Brussels sprouts, potatoes, Kalamata olives with lemon, herbs and seasonings. It was phenomenal. I don't know that I'd ever really tasted food before. To me everything tasted like American cheese or ranch dressing with hints of other things. This was a cacophony of flavors exploding in my mouth.

Katie had a lot to teach me about food that summer. Now true to my roots I didn't give up meat altogether, but I did learn to add flavor to my food in more creative ways. Who knew that guacamole is the most amazing cheese substitute on a burger? Or that adding a fried egg to a Reuben in lieu of Swiss was good enough to bring on a When Harry Met Sally moment at dinner one night. And my new diet made me so mindful of what I put into my body. But it wasn't until I took a trip back to Texas that I realized how much I had changed.

"Don't turn sideways or you'll disappear," my old buddy Rachel told me.

Not only was I tasting real food, but I was feeling better and I had lost a ton of fat and flab. I hadn't seen those numbers on the scale since high school, and it felt great.

Now some people did pity me for having to cut out all dairy just to nurse my young. And I caught a lot of heat for nursing my daughter when she was able to walk and talk. But I found it funny that they thought I was the weirdo for letting her have milk from my teat instead of a doe-eyed bovine.

Eventually Sunny did stop nursing, and I was free to indulge in my dairy treats once more. And since this isn't a story about a hero, I'm not ashamed to say that I did fall off the wagon and went out for Coldstone with my good buddy Amber.

I am however ashamed to say that I spent that night shivering naked on the bathroom floor because of my dairy indiscretions. The milk gods were not kind that night, but I did develop a tolerance for dairy once more.

However now that baby Violet has arrived I'm taking no chances. I don't want her to suffer like her big sis, so once again I have sworn off the moo juice once again just in case. But this time there was no detox phase and I know now that pepper is a seasoning, garlic is a flavor and the sacred cow no longer has reign over the happiness of my taste buds.

Hobby Lobby Lessons

Part of my job description as a mom is to teach my kids right from wrong. A wise soul once told me that children are little uncivilized people. They are people, so they have valid feelings and a voice to be heard. But they need to be civilized, and part of teaching that civilization is guiding their moral compass. Unfortunately some children miss that lesson and grow up to be hoodlums who get run down by minivans in the Hobby Lobby parking lot.

Yesterday my friend Mary and I took a trip to the Lobby just to browse all the potential Pinterest projects that wonderful store has to offer. We loaded up the kids in the "I've given up" wagon, a.k.a. my minivan, and headed to the craft store.

We rounded up our loot, and as Mary was checking out with her 15 giant discounted picture frames, my toddler and I went to pull the van around front. But while strapping Violet into her car seat I saw something sparkly in her grubby little paw.

She'd boosted a pretty awesome Little Mermaid scepter from the toy kiosk near the register. It was only a $2 toy, and I was in a little bit of a hurry. It would have been easy to just let her keep the silly thing. The only alarm bells that sounded were the ones in my head that said, "Stealing is wrong. Teach your toddler."

Well the only thing Violet thought I was trying to teach her was that Mommy is mean and takes awesome princess scepters from little children. But my good deed did not go unnoticed by my 4-year-old.

"Violet, we do not take toys without paying," she scolded. I beamed a little as I jogged back inside to return the stolen merchandise.

I walked in and announced "Looks like we have a shoplifter." All the cashiers' heads whipped around and one guy near the candy kiosk looked up in a panic. I casually laughed, waved the scepter and explained what happened.

The cashier thanked me for my honesty, so I smiled, laid the scepter down on the counter and jogged back to the car.

Mary and I giggled about my little thief as I buckled up, but as I put the van in gear a guy came barreling out of the store followed by the manager and the nice stock boy who had helped us load the frames into my van. It was the candy kiosk guy, and his jacket was full of stolen merchandise.

The middle-aged manager and the little stock boy were huffing and puffing, but the thief was way ahead of them. He knew that he could outrun those guys, but what he didn't know is that he could not outrun a certain mother driving a minivan with a breastfeeding bumper sticker. If I wouldn't let my toddler get away with stealing a prized Ariel scepter I certainly wouldn't let this thug muffin steal some crafting goods.

I put the pedal to the metal and floored it through the parking lot after this kid who only looked back once to see the distance growing between him and the Hobby Lobby employees. As I got closer to the thief I wasn't sure of my intentions. I wasn't going to murder him for stealing some curly ribbon, but I couldn't just let him get away either. So I laid on my horn frantically and got right on his tail.

I can't even describe his face as he turned around to see a minivan full of kids and moms about to take him out. His eyes went wide in surprise, confusion and that look you get when you know you've been caught doing something bad by your momma. He threw his jacket in the air and packages of markers and cans of spray paint went flying into a nearby cactus. I think he was rethinking his style choices as he tried to pull up his sagging jeans and bolted into oncoming traffic. He channeled his inner Frogger and made it across the street safely, but he didn't even turn around as he kept running through the gas station parking lot and out of sight.

The winded manager approached the van fighting back laughter until he saw that he'd be picking merchandise out of a cactus. He thanked us for our help as our kids cheered from the back. Although we didn't catch him, I'd like to think that thief might have learned a small lesson. After all he did have to go explain to his cohorts that he didn't get the goods because some crazy little blonde lady in a minivan scared him almost clean out of his pants.

Southern Fried Renegade

So I did the unthinkable and I spent a week with my in-laws sans husband. But before you gasp, seize and pass out please realize that they are not evil monstrous beings hell-bent on making my life miserable. On the contrary they spoil me and my beloved daughter rotten, so it's actually quite fun going and lounging by the pool, strolling through New Orleans munching on beignets and having three square meals set before me that I didn't have to prepare.

My father-in-law married a good Southern woman who is the polar opposite of me, and that's probably why we get along swimmingly. Yes dear readers, if you happen to have read my previous columns (So pretty much just my editor because he has to and my Nana because she's retired), this is the same mother-in-law who is a completely neurotic neat freak. But even if she reads this she'll thank me for the compliment.

Of course as in every visit my dear mother-in-law tries to whip her poor daughter-in-law into a proper Southern belle. Even though my own mama did put me through cotillion, and I attended a bona fide coming out party, I just ain't quite polished enough. So my dear sweet mother-in-law periodically gives me her essential Southern girl lecture, during which I am reminded of the Five Commandments of all good Southern women. Mankind needs ten, but good Southern ladies can do twice as good with half as many.

Number one, thou shalt keep a spotless house, lest your neighbors gossip at your deserved expense. My mother-in-law holds this law above all others. Not only could you eat off of her floors, but should you choose to dine a la laminate your gut would probably get a good scrubbing from the cleaning fairies that live in the pores of her woodwork.

Number two, thou shalt never go to the grocery store without full make-up and hair done. Lord only knows who you'll run into there, and we must always look our best.

Number three, thou shalt not eat full fat foods. A good Southern girl should really only taste and pick at the food she is preparing for her guests and or rich handsome husband. If she does have a meal it should consist of the fewest calories possible. Chubby was only cute back in the middle ages.

Number four, thou shalt use the lessons learned in commandments one through three to attract a rich handsome husband. According to the written word, Southern gentlemen care about three things, a clean house, a good meal and a skinny beautiful wife to make it happen. My poor husband really got a raw deal on that one. As far as trophy wives go, I'd say I'm more of an honorable mention.

Number five, if ever a Southern girl forgets her commandments, it is the duty of her fellow belles to gossip...er, um...discuss what can be done to help the poor soul. However if one must speak unkindly of another belle, she need only say "Bless her heart." As in "Margaret has become such a cow, bless her heart." It shows compassion for the poor soul who has fallen from Southern grace. Also accepted is "I love her but," as in "Now I love Catharine, but her house was a mess."

Now bless my mother-in-law's heart, I will never be a good Southern Belle. In my defense I was born and raised in Texas, and they do it a little different. Yes they like the big hair and full makeup just like the rest of those Southern gals. I do sleep with one eye open while I'm visiting lest they bleach ambush my hair again.

But they also amended Southern commandment one to replace good housekeeping with a well-paid cleaning woman. Number two still stands with the full hair and face at the grocery, but number three can kiss a pork butt. We love us some barbecue, and my husband fell in love with me when I kept up with him at all-you-can-eat wing night. Number four and five don't even register in a Texas girl's book because we're raised with a little more grit and rattlesnake venom than the belles. There's no need to gossip behind another girl's back because a Texas girl has no problem speaking her mind. We brawl it out, brood over it a minute and move on to the next confrontation, which is usually our husbands or best friend.

And rather than trying to convince some guy that we're worth their time and money, a Texas girl knows that the point of a husband is to have someone who tells you how gorgeous you are and nod and smile when spoken to. Now I guess since I don't quite fit the trophy wife bit, I can't very well expect my husband to let me completely rule the roost. I strayed away a bit and married a guy with a bull head and a strong backbone. But he does have a way of making me feel like a beauty queen even when I'm 12 months pregnant and swollen like a pig with a bee sting.

So I headed home from my visit to Southern Lady academy feeling refreshed and semi-polished. And I will admit that when I got home I did a load of dishes and tidied up the living room. But then I threw my hair in a ponytail and headed to the grocery with only a little mascara to get myself a big steak for the grill.

Pickles on Display

This was submitted to Our Town magazine, but we decided it was a little morbid for our family friendly publication.

So I heard about this guy with a very creepy hobby. Apparently this fella takes dead human bodies and dresses them up. Yeah we're talking full makeup, hair done, and then he basically plays paper dolls with them and puts them in fancy clothes like they're having tea with the Queen. He puts the corpses out on display and people can actually come admire his work just like the lopsided clay pot your daughter made for the 4th grade open house. Very Norman Bates of him. But the sick thing is that people actually flock to gawk at this odd sort of taxidermy.

The guy hasn't gotten in trouble with the law, and it's safe to say that you've probably seen his, or some of his colleagues' handiwork. The folks who participate in this freaky fetish are typically called morticians. Now one can't really fault the morticians, after all they are merely performing a service that our weirdo society has a need for. The crazy looks should be directed at ourselves for participating in such a messed up tradition.

I recently attended my great-grandmother's funeral, and I couldn't help but be repulsed by the very idea of going to gaze upon her ashen face. Last time I saw her she looked radiant in her yellow blouse with matching yellow slacks and cheery smile. Of course my family thought I was just cold and either wasn't dealing with her death properly, or I just couldn't possibly have loved her as they did. Since some of them even went as far as to kiss her cold carcass. But I just don't see how ogling her lifeless body would help prove my love for her. I thought the birthday cards, photos and letters I sent her meant something. But still I had family members quite literally dragging me up to the coffin for "closure."

Well funny thing about the word closure. I feel like when you die we should just close yer casket and be done with it. Matter of fact, I really don't see the point of a casket. There's padding. Seriously has there ever been a customer complaint filed about the weird bar poking them in the back? Negative.

I just don't need to see some old body parts pumped full of chemicals to know that they're gone. It would take a pretty sick person to call me up and say, "Hey your 86-year-old great-grandmother passed peacefully in her sleep." Only later to call and say "April Fools!" No, I'm quite convinced that when I get the news that a loved one has passed, I'll buy it. Maybe I'm just gullible that way.

To me, saying goodbye to a flesh pile is not the same as saying goodbye to a flesh pile that can talk back. I lost so many family members unexpectedly when I was young, so I've learned to say goodbye as if it's the last time...every time. Of course with those old folks you never know how long they'll hang in there. Eighty-six is a ripe old age, so maybe I do hug the older crowd a little tighter. But you never know with those young folks either. Disease strikes, four-wheelers crash and stuff happens. None of us are guaranteed to be old and wrinkly corpses. Some of us get in that casket without support hose and bingo wings.

But no matter the age, the thing that freaks me out is when people say, "Oh she looked beautiful." Really? Really now? That motionless heap up there that used to be a living, breathing, passionate, funny woman with her Ph.D. and a penchant for world travels, looked good? Sorry, but I think they look better when they're bustling around the kitchen making the world's best stir fry.

Instead of fawning over these useless skin sacks why don't we throw a party to celebrate the good times? And I don't mean the kind that follows the funeral where Aunt Jillian brings her best Jell-O salad and everyone sits around talking about anything but the dearly departed. I mean throw a shindig with tons of photos of the deceased before they bought the farm.

Talk about their accomplishments, or just about the time they tickled you until you peed.

It's sick that we try to hang onto the dead for just a little longer by pumping their bodies full of preservatives. Come on, as if that person never ate a McDouble. They're preserved enough. Just throw them in the backyard and fertilize a new flower garden in their honor. It's pretty messed up that it's illegal to just bury your husband in the backyard (believe me, I've come close so I checked some city ordinances), but it's perfectly within the law to drain his fluids, put makeup on him, pump him full of chemicals and put him on display for a few days. That's just weird.

So when I go dear readers, please don't buy me a new outfit and a death bed that costs more than my car. Either burn me up so I'm not taking up precious space that could be used for a Chuck E. Cheese. Or, just give my body to science. It could be fun if I ended up as a practice dummy for a plastic surgeon. I'd rather be Misses Potato Head after I'm gone than a useless pickle on display.

Mama's Hot Date

When I got married I figured I was done with the dating scene. We settled in nicely with couple friends, and once we decided to have kids I knew my dating days were over. But about six months after my darling Sunny was born I found myself getting ready for a date. My first playdate.

In the early days of her birth I wasn't ready to meet anyone. I was still getting used to my new motherly status. The childfree days of staying out late or sleeping in past - well sleeping at all - those days were over. And slowly the divide between me and my childless friends started to widen. It's not that I didn't love them anymore, but they weren't in a place in their lives where barf on their shirt was a sign of affection, and they just didn't share my concern about the quantity or consistency of my offspring's bowel movements.

The first few months of motherhood were a little lonely. But it gave me time to grieve for the childfree life I left behind. I didn't expect to mourn it so much, and although that sweet little cherub did capture my heart I still longed for the days of eating lunch when I felt like it and going to the bathroom by myself. Yes a person was quite literally attached to me most of the day, but I couldn't help feeling a little stranded on this baby island.

Then about six months after my sweet one was born I started to shower and put on real pants. I was ready to get out there again and make some new friends. Someone I could talk to about my sudden irrational obsession with hand sanitizer or share my deepest confessions about who I was secretly sharing my bed with.

In college making friends came easy. Between work and school I had all sorts of social avenues to sift through. But now that I was out of the working world and only going to Target a few times a week it was a little tougher to meet new people.

I ventured into the mama dating world gently by asking the interwebs for help. I found a few local moms groups online and started internet dating them. I would check out their Meetup.com profiles to weed out the weirdos and find some thread of similarities that I might bond with. Instead of looking for someone with blue eyes and a strong chin, I found myself getting excited over our kids sharing a birth month or the vegan mom I could swap dairy-free recipes with.

Another great avenue I found was the mommy singles bar, also known as the playground. Moms will casually saunter up with their little ones in tow, and as the children scamper off to the slides the mommies mill about the cedar mulch dance floor or take a break at the picnic table wet bar.

Some great pickup lines I learned were, "Where did you get that baby carrier?" or "Oh how precious. How old is he?" This line is a great opener because if your kids are close in age and she doesn't seem like a freak you could be meeting your new best friend. The playground is also a great neutral ground to see how the kids play together. If her kid is constantly shoving your kid's face in the dirt at the playground you can pretty much write off the friendship. It won't get any better when you bring your kid to her kid's home turf.

I started to feel more comfortable in my mommy dating world. And then came my first blind date. My husband played ball with her husband, our girls were born just a few months apart, and the best part was she was super lonely. Jackpot.

I asked her husband for her number one day at softball practice, and I can't say my palms weren't sweaty as I dialed her number later that evening. I nervously laughed and made a witty off-the-cuff suggestion that we should get together since we popped out our kids at roughly the same time and she agreed.

I spent half an hour picking an outfit for myself. I needed something cute but not too revealing so that I could nurse discreetly if I had to. After all I was going to her house and I didn't want to give the wrong impression by whipping my boobs out on the first date. I probably spent another half hour picking an outfit for Sunny. I wanted her to look cute, but not like Toddlers and Tiaras cute.

As I lugged my infant seat up to the door and fumbled with my giant diaper bag my heart started to pound. What if I couldn't think of anything to talk about? What if her kid chewed on my kid's teething ring? But as the door opened our eyes met, she smiled and Sunny ripped a huge fart. She cracked up, ushered me in and I didn't leave until her husband strolled in the door at 6 p.m.

It had been scary, exciting and downright exhausting to get back out there in the dating world, and I met lots of moms I would be wonderful friends with. But the day of my first blind playdate I knew I'd met The One.

The Dragon Mom

My little Sunny always has big plans for her future. Some days she wants to be a veterinarian, and others she wants to be a dragon. As her mom it's my job to help her achieve all she desires. A vet may be easier than the dragon thing, but we'll cross that bridge when we get there.

So yesterday, when she explained that she was going to be a pediatrician and a professional athlete while her husband stayed at home to be a daddy, I couldn't help but feel a little proud. As a stay-at-home mom I've always been a little worried that she might not realize the opportunities women have now to "have it all."

I realize I'm lucky for the luxury of staying at home with my darlings. Some moms have to get back to the grind when their wee ones are only weeks old. And I am truly grateful that I was there for the first steps and words and blinks and poops and all the wonders of those magical baby years. But there has always been that part of me that was itching for the working world. A part that craves a different kind of responsibility and a different kind of reward. Sure those sweet sticky kisses are a fine reward for putting enough jelly on the

PBJ, but that paycheck sure was a nice thank you for a job well done.

So as my stay-at-home journey nears its end I'm starting to get excited at the prospect of going back to grown up world. I'm sure I'm looking back with rose colored glasses, for I faintly remember feeling a bit like a prisoner on particularly sunny days when I was cooped up in an office instead of the freedom of the swing set at the park. But there are so many things that I look forward to that the working world offers. Lunch breaks, for instance. I think I remember a very fast 45-ish minutes of freedom where I could cut my own food and eat it while it was hot. I think I even remember going to the bathroom by myself, but I could be wrong.

I told my mother-in-law, a retired teacher, that I was perusing the job boards, and she wondered what school I was looking to teach at. I politely explained that the path of the educator was not in my future, and she was horrified. What would I do with the children after school and during summer break? Certainly not – gulp – daycare?

The truth is I don't know. I'm taking a pretty decent hiatus from my career to pour my heart and soul into my kids. I'm trying to give them the best running start so that when they get to elementary school, and I'm back at work full-time they will have had so much quality time with me they want to puke and will welcome the break. Quite frankly, if we've had the better part of five years together one on one, the quality of our time together will probably start to decline.

I'm a mom that needs to work. It's why I never gave up writing. I needed an outlet, a peephole into the working world. And although most of my "work" involves writing about children, it's still my portal into the professional arena. Some moms don't need that outlet. They pour everything they have into running the household, and I am certainly not one to scoff at such an undertaking.

To some moms having it all means spending as much time at home with the kids and keeping the house running full tilt. To some it's setting an example as a thriving career woman. And for some like me having it all is somewhere in between. There's so much judgment between women for choices as big as being a "working" or "stay-at-home" mom, and for choices as small as diaper brands. Instead of judgment we should all just acknowledge what a freaking hard job it is just to keep children alive. Doesn't it seem like they think they're constantly on hidden camera for Fear Factor?

So even if my girls are in some sort of after-school program or have to trade off weeks with Grammy and Mimi during the summer, I think they'll survive. In fact they'll more than survive. They'll see their mom as more than a lady who burns the eggs and replenishes the bath towels. They'll see me as the strong independent woman I want them to know they can be. A role model who can pursue her passion while still burning eggs for the ones she holds dear.

And one day when Dr. Sunny is taking care of baby dragons in between her responsibilities to the WNBA, her husband will shift my grandchild to his hip and give me a high five for teaching his wife that she can have it all.

Ghosts of Halloweens Past

This year I was put in charge of my MOMS Club Halloween Open House, which I was completely pumped about since Halloween is one of my absolute favorite holidays, second only maybe to Thanksgiving. Who doesn't love eating five different starches in the name of tradition?

I couldn't wait to rock this event, since last year's shindig was less than spectacular in my opinion. Picture a giant empty room in the basement of a church with no decorations and only folding table with rinky dink face painting going on. There was also an area where kids could use glue sticks to paste black construction paper on paper plates and call them pumpkins, but it was mainly filled with bored or crying children. Scary, but not in the good Halloweeny way.

This is supposed to entice people to join our club, and I was ready to spice this thing up like a hot cider. However as I had visions of sugar pops and spider webs dancing in my head, I got an email from the President. No big B.O. didn't give me a shout; it was from our MOMS Club president laying out some "suggestions" for the party. And by suggestions I mean the law since she's the prez.

I was told to make sure we didn't do anything too scary for the little children who might be terrified of things like witches and ghosts. She named her five-year-old as one of the scaredy cats, but I'm honestly more terrified of that child than Chucky. I was also instructed not to have candy or little toys as treats or prizes, since none of the mothers need any of that at the house. And I also need to stick to things like pumpkins and hay bales as decorations. Anything too Halloween-related might offend some of our more religious party guests.

So let me get this straight, we are to have a Halloween party with no candy, no witches or ghosts, or anything that could be deemed scary or religiously offensive. We are to have pumpkins and hay bales, and judging from last year's festivities, we are also allowed to transform various paper products into one of those two items. This just isn't the Halloween I remember as a kid.

Now I was raised by a devout Christian mother. She dragged my sleepy butt out of bed on Sunday mornings to attend Sunday school and then even made my growling stomach sit through Big Church. But come October, she was not only sewing elaborate costumes for my brother and me, but she donned disguises herself.

We went trick or treating and were allowed to eat all the candy we wanted in one night. Since I had some sort of brain sickness, I always traded my brother my candy for his butler services. And Mom would let me trade candy for fruits and veggies, since I preferred those. But my brother gorged himself on Twizzlers, Snickers and even those gross orange and black peanut butter ones that most kids just pelt each other with outside.

Our house was decked with ghosts and witches and candlesticks with cobwebs that lit up when you walked by. And each year we'd carve our jack-o-lanterns and roast the seeds while we watched scary movies in the dark. It was good times, and there was nothing sacrilegious about it.

Now I wasn't planning to have Freddy Krueger chase the children into a pit of snakes, but could a few green witches with little black cats really offend anyone? And would it really be a crime if the kids could win a Tootsie Roll at one of the game stations I'd imagined? We could even make it a pumpkin bean bag toss to appease the pumpkin gods that ruled over last year's events.

I just don't see the harm in a little Halloween fun. I mean after all, it started as a religious holiday. It was the day when the dead could return to the earth, and that's the religious folks' idea. I wasn't planning to have zombies running around; I just wanted some cauldrons with hot cider and a few toy bats and spiders. I just don't see why my childhood Halloween traditions have become so not P.C. Kids need to suck it up a little if they're afraid of a few paper ghosts and a cartoony looking Frankenstein. My two-year-old pulls scarier things out of her diaper.

I think maybe I'll plan my event the way I want to do it. I'll set it up myself and no one will be the wiser until the frightening fiasco is unveiled complete with sugary treats and maybe even a germ infested drowning hazard like bobbing for apples. And if they hate it, then I'm banned from planning any future events and possibly stripped of my mother-of-the-year trophy. But maybe, just maybe, the smell of popcorn balls and candy corn will ignite a childhood spark they forgot about. And they'll see some ghosts from their Halloween pasts that aren't so scary after all.

Laundry and Flesh Wounds

Today as I looked at the calendar I realized two things. The first was that it is the drop dead deadline for my column, and that I should probably kiss my wonderfully forgiving editors behind. The other is that tomorrow is my birthday.

Deadlines that creep up on me are nothing new. But birthdays are something to be anticipated for weeks in advance. See I'm not one of those girls who dreads her birthaversary. I've tried to be demure and pretend that it's just another day. "Pish posh. Don't fuss over me." And I've tried to be the girl who just can't believe she's that much closer to the dreaded 3-0. Worrying about crow's feet and wrinkles. But in all honesty I am so not that girl. I am the girl who freaking loves her birthday.

Maybe it's narcissism, or maybe it's that I'm just a perpetual 6-year-old. Either way, I totally relish the fact that there is one day out of the year that is all my own. The rest of the year I consider myself a pretty thoughtful person. I love making other people feel important and special for 364 days in a row. But there is one day a year that I do milk for all it's worth.

I am the person who doesn't do laundry on her birthday. I refuse to have doctor's appointments or any other nonsense that might interfere with my queen bee status. Even if no one else decides to spoil me, I will strut around with an air of superiority for 24 glorious hours because dang it it's my birthday.

So as I sit here toiling away, watching the clock tick down to midnight, I can't figure out how this birthday got away from me. I'm not afraid to admit that this is my last year in my 20s. I won't be celebrating my 29th birthday over and over as some ladies choose to do. I've been married almost a decade and I've got two wonderfully crazy children who have aged me far more than any old birthday could do. But is it possible though that I've outgrown my girlish love of myself and the sacredness of this one special day?

I looked at my calendar for tomorrow to see if I had any fun birthtivities planned. But horror of horrors the only thing on the agenda is a minor skin surgery to remove a "cluster of abnormal cells." And to top it off I have to finish my laundry in the morning because my baby goose has swim lessons, and her swim suit is in the wash. Laundry and flesh wounds. That will be my 29th birthday.

I woke my husband up to inform him of these grave circumstances, and he assured me that my birthday is in fact Saturday. I told him to go back to sleep before I cause him bodily harm. He forgot my birthday too!

Normally I would have demanded justice. There should be a feast in my honor prepared by the townsfolk weeks in advance so that I know that for one day I am the center of the gall dern universe. But as I was sulking out of the room I heard a little whimper and saw a tiny hand in the moonlight reaching for my pillow. For my totally loyal readers, you'll know already that I let my children sleep in my bed. This is no time for lectures. I've made peace with it, and so should you.

As those little whimpers got more persistent I rushed back to bed to cuddle up to my little Violet. She snuggled up to nurse and I melted into her sweet little chubby hands. Hubs threw his big lug arm over me and mumbled something about being an idiot and of course he knew tomorrow was my birthday. So I laid there in the arms of my big oaf while cuddling my tiny tot. And soon after I heard the pitter patter of little feet running down the stairs and into my room. Without uttering a word my sleepy little Sunny girl climbed into bed in between the Hubs and I and buried her sweet little face in the crook of my neck.

I knew I had to get up and write my column, but I just had to lay there and soak in that sweet moment. And then I realized how the day snuck up on me. My life is filled with days where I am the end all be all to three of the most wonderful people on earth. I'm important and special and loved 364 days in a row. So a little fanfare on that one day makes less of a difference since I have such awesome admirers year-round.

That being said if there's no cake tomorrow I know three precious heads that will roll. A girl deserves a little extra sweetness just once a year.

The Last Donut

Thursday mornings are a magical time for me. I drop my little spud off at preschool and head over to a hole-in-the wall called Donuts N' Coffee. This little slice of heaven serves up respite in the form of sugary soft hoops of ecstasy. I typically opt for the Homer Simpson as I call it, which is a fluffy little cake donut topped with pink flavored icing and sprinkles. Yes pink is a flavor.

I settle into one of the orange and brown booths, whip out my Kindle and sink into oblivion surrounded by wood paneling and the warm conversation of the only other patrons who share my Thursday morning sanctuary: The Ol' Codger Table.

This little band of six older gentlemen is there each Thursday morning to lend wisdom and a sympathetic ear to one another. They move from politics to cataracts without blinking. I'm sure their wives are either at home or no longer with them. That subject never seems to come up. It's all business with this group, and although I typically tune them out as I delve into the pages of my latest brain candy, I couldn't help but listen in this morning.

Tom, one of the more frequent topic pickers of the group, decided this morning's agenda needed to include discussion of his doctor's insistence that he is getting old. Apparently his physician discovered a serious problem with his prostate that he feels to be of the utmost importance. The other gentlemen concurred that indeed their doctors had also informed them that they needed this or that operated on or that this number wasn't quite what it needed to be. But none of them seemed to agree with the whippersnapper docs who think they know the length of time they have left on their tickers.

In the midst of each of them taking their turn telling what ailments they were bravely battling, Bud found it pertinent to mention that the apple critters were particularly moist this morning, and Leon noted that it was lucky they'd been wise enough to nab their treats early, as Barbara appeared to be completely sold out of everything save for one lone cruller. The conversation of deadly disorders vanished into compliments on the coffee and cinnamon rolls without a hitch.

I smiled to myself as they moved fluidly from talking about the subject of their imminent demise to being thankful they'd gotten the last long john. I marveled at these six men surely in the dead winter of their lives, who talked as if squeaking by with the last bag of donut holes was a closer call than their bout with cancer last year.

Now I'm probably borderline hypochondriac, so I can imagine that if some young doctor told me I had some sort of life-threatening illness I'd be making a bucket list and going to the deepest part of the Amazon searching for a cure. I took the news gravely when I found out I had pregnancy-induced anemia and just needed to take an iron supplement. I've even been lying awake at night going through all the potential scenarios that may or may not come up now that I'm going to be a mother of two. Anxiety has me wide awake at 4 a.m. for things that might not ever be. So it begs to reason that maybe these old geezers have the right attitude.

None of us really knows when the bell will toll for us. They probably each have a list of battle scars from all the bad hands life can deal. They've been through the gauntlet enough times with friends and loved ones to really understand the concept of that which doesn't kill us makes us stronger. So one silly doctor telling them that the boogie man lives in their colon isn't going to phase them.

As Bud sipped his coffee and the subject moved to the upcoming election, I sank back down into my book. I feel lucky to share the donut shop and my Thursday mornings with these suspender-sporting sages. They've reminded me to just savor the sweet stuff when you can, because you never know if that donut is the last one.

Cowboys and Indians

Last night I went to a Diwali celebration and was one of only maybe 10 pale faces in a sea of a thousand Indians. It was dinner and a show, and they were all dressed in the beautifully ornate traditional garb of their culture. The hubs told me he got tickets at the last minute, and all I really knew of Diwali was from a hilarious, yet less-than-educational episode of The Office. So naturally when I got there and saw the level of elegance that most were exuding, I felt quite underwhelming in my classic black on grey attire.

But as I sat in the audience watching the vibrant dancers on stage leaping and swooping to the joyful music, I felt so grateful to the people around me for their hospitality and willingness to share such a special piece of their culture with me.

I grew up in small-town Texas, where you might be surprised to learn has an incredibly limited Indian population. I only ever knew one boy of Indian descent who was in a few of my classes in junior high. Ethnic diversity is not Odessa's forte. Giant jackrabbits and prairie dogs we have, ethnic diversity we have not. It's pretty much Texans, and people who ain't from 'round here.

Now Texans can be any color you please, but you have to be born within the borders of the state. Think of the border between Texas and Mexico as more of a dotted line, and the border between Texas and Oklahoma is an impenetrable force field.

Texans are proud as a people. We even have our own toast, and things are absolutely bigger there. All my exes live there and the oil industry is bigger than Kevin Bacon since everyone there is connected to it in less than seven degrees.

But the food. Oh the food. The Mexican food is what I miss the most about my childhood home. Florida has Cuban food, and it is totally spectacular. But it's like comparing manzanas and naranjas. They're just not the same. The Hubs is from New Orleans, so he's pretty proud of his jambalaya and red beans and rice. But his pride is nothing next to a Texan's.

Food to me is the spokes model of a culture. It's what represents the heart and soul of the people and it relies on nature to provide the flavors that showcase that region of the earth. And as a Texan I like to proudly declare that our food is superior to all others. It's the playground taunt of 'My dad is stronger than your dad.' Food is a source of pride for each culture, but it's also a way to bring us together.

As the Diwali dancers neared their finale last night, tendrils of mouthwatering aromas crept through the theater. It was almost time for dinner, and I was starving. I knew not to expect enchiladas, but aside from that I was going in blind.

As we walked through the buffet line, my little blonde-haired blue-eyed toddler danced wildly without reservation mimicking the Diwali performers as the young Indian woman next to me chuckled warmly. Her mother smiled sweetly at my silly dancer and said something to me in a language I didn't understand. Her daughter told me her mother said that my daughter reminded her of her own granddaughter, who came running up just a few moments later.

The little girl had bells on her ankles and was decked head to toe in pink and gold. She and Sunny briefly sized each other up before squealing with delight and whirling around as the music drifted through the dining hall. Her big beautiful brown eyes and dark hair were a stark comparison to my little cherub, but the woman was right. As they whirled around squealing it was clear to see that they were just two different flavors of the same cookie.

We sat down near their family so the girls could play, and as we ate I felt more and more accepted. I was so obviously an outsider, someone who wouldn't know a sari from a dhoti, but each gaze was met with a smile and a nod. An acknowledgement that I was welcome to break bread with these people who seemed so different from my family.

But as I devoured fork after fork of tikka masala, naan and biryani my insecurities melted away. We were just people. We're all representatives of mankind. We all have the same heart and soul. And the best way to mankind's heart is through his stomach.

Room to Grow

At 9:30 a.m. I called my husband and said, "I'm not sure, but I think I might be in labor." I couldn't time my contractions because my toddler was distracting me with her shenanigans. And when the contractions got stronger and I tried to roll on the birthing ball for relief, my toddler decided I should suck it up and stole the ball right out from under me. Realizing that I might actually be in labor, and being in no mood for distractions, I called my friend to come and get Sunny for a play date while I figured out if I was about to have a baby.

As I gathered her things in between contractions I was still in pretty deep denial that I was in labor. It only made sense because I think I was in denial about having another child throughout my pregnancy. I was overtaken with emotions that ranged from pure joy to guilt. I was elated to be pregnant. I'm one of the weirdos who actually likes being preggers. I was happy that our family would be complete, and I was overjoyed when we found out it was another girl. I'd always wanted a sister, so I was very excited that my daughter would have one. But most of my pregnancy emotions were directly tied to Sunny, my first-born.

I'd planned and plotted and wished and dreamed and did everything short of voodoo to get pregnant with my oldest child. This second pregnancy snuck up on me a few days after we celebrated Sunny's second birthday. We'd always planned on two, but we certainly weren't trying when that little stick turned pink. I'd planned to wait until Sunny was 5, so that I would have enough one-on-one time with her. Then when she was in school I'd welcome another baby. But my ovaries had other plans. And I felt guilty for that. How could I possibly find time for Sunny if I was glued to an infant? And would I have enough love for the both of them?

As I kissed Sunny goodbye I savored the moment. Deep down I knew that was our last morning as a duo, and the moment was bittersweet. But just two hours later I held Violet Elyse in my arms.

In the time Before Violet, or BV as I now refer to it, Sunny and I spent our days at the park, reading books or having picnics in the backyard. The world revolved around her. If she wanted to sit at the library for three hours, then so be it. If we wanted to make pancakes at 3 p.m. we made them. And each day at nap time I snuggled up next to her and read stories until we fell asleep. I felt so guilty for taking that away because I knew when Violet came that those days were over.

Maybe that guilt came from knowing what it was like to be the older child when a new baby comes home. I was queen bee of the universe for five glorious years before my baby brother showed up. And since he was three months premature he got loads of attention that was formerly reserved only for me. I remember feeling resentful and jealous, and I didn't want that for my daughter. Plus I kept feeling guilty about the new baby because I wasn't sure I could ever love anyone as much as I love my Sunny.

Then, on her daddy's birthday, our little Violet came into the world. Sunny's labor and delivery was horrible. It was a slow and painful induction. I had an epidural and pushed for three hours. When she finally came I was so wiped and numb that I could hardly process what was happening. But Violet's labor happened so fast, and Sunny distracted me so well through the toughest part, that there was no time for the epidural. I brought Vi into the world without so much as a Tylenol, and it was the most invigorating and emotional experience of my life.

As they placed that warm little body on my chest I wept, and I understood how I could love her every bit as much as Sunny. My heart wasn't big enough for the two of them, but when Violet was born my heart grew. I'm sure I didn't feel it, what with all the contractions, but my heart must have sprouted a new corridor.

The reason you can love the second as much as the first is the same reason you can love your husband and your mother and your friends. Because each person who comes into your life and deserves your love gets their own spot. It's the reason that when a loved one passes away or a friend moves across the country you say "They'll always have a special place in my heart."

Because they do. And Violet was busy constructing her own little spot in utero. I'm sure that's what all that kicking and bustling around was about. I was under construction. Your children get the biggest and best spots because they're so close to the source for nine months. I'm sure Violet set hers up right next to Sunny's because already I can see the love between them.

And as I watch Sunny dote on her new baby sister, I realize what a gift I've given her. Violet isn't some thief here to steal the limelight and my love. She's a sister and a lifelong friend who I'm sure already has her own special place in Sunny's heart.

High School Sweetheart

A sure-fire sign of my elderly status has arrived in the form of an invitation to my 10-year high school reunion. It seems the Permian Panther class of 2002 will be reuniting in June to reconnect with one another through totally non-judgmental cocktails and conversation.

I swore when I graduated that there was no way I'd go to my reunion. I figured it was just for losers who were still trying to cling to their glory days and band nerds who like to creep around the band hall years after graduation. I would be much too busy with my career to even bother with those cretins. But for whatever reason I'm a little intrigued now that it's actually upon me.

Now I really have no business going. Let's put aside the fact that the reunion is scheduled a mere three months after I'll have given birth to my second child, and therefore I will arrive as a flabby pile of stretch-marked wonderment. I will undoubtedly have to field questions about when the baby is due, for surely my uterus will betray me and not contract back down until weeks after the reunion, giving me the super sexy appearance of being 5 months with child.

But there's no sense in dwelling on that. I've heard from one source that we have at least 11 people from our graduating class who are also expecting within a month or two of me, so there's to be one or two other fatties.

But lay the cards out. Everyone knows that the 10-year reunion is the one you attend to measure your self-worth against people you vaguely remember and only occasionally Facebook stalk when you're bored or avoiding deadlines at 3 a.m. And I'm just not where I thought I'd be.

I imagined that if I graced those urchins with my presence I'd be a mega successful journalist living in the big city. No friggin' way I'd be tied down to a husband or needy little ankle biters.

But as it stands I'm a stay-at-home mom with one ankle biter on the outside and one planning its escape from the womb. I'm not even a hardcore single mom who had artificial insemination because my career was too time-consuming for me to date. Nope. I have a stupid husband who I actually think is pretty awesome. We live in the burbs, I secretly envy those with minivans, and one of my sources of great pride is our 15-year mortgage we just refinanced on our 1964 ranch-style home. Yippee.

I know I technically have a job as a freelancer. And my responsibility to dazzle the 5 people who read my column and the super newsworthy articles I write on vacationing on a dime do get me a technical "employed" status. But there are idiots I graduated with who are really actually working grown-up jobs where they fly out of town on business and wear pants when they work.

What do I tell those snotty brats when they ask in a honey sweet voice of condescension, "So do you just stay home with the kids now?" as they text super important business things on their iPhones.

Yep it's just me and my muumuu all day. I used to take me a smoke break to get away from the kids, but then the macaronies burnt up and my old man gets all steamed. So I just drink to drown out the noise and the pain of my life choices.

Now I did graduate from quite the prestigious university (cough, Go Gators, cough). So that does account for something. And a journalism degree from said university is nothing to sneeze at. And although many of my J-School peers are living out dreams of writing in the big city, I have to humbly admit that I'm satisfied with the path my life took.

I had all the plans in the world of being Miss Independent Career Woman. It's why I moved a thousand miles from Little Town, Texas all the way to

Florida without knowing a soul in the state. I'd planned to just get my college on a bit and then head off to NYU to complete my journalism degree. But instead of whisking away to The Big Apple or D.C. to be some hard-hitting reporter, I fell in love. I fell in love with my husband; I fell in love with Florida; and I fell in love with magazine writing.

I didn't know it, but all my plans of who I thought I would be in 10 years went out the window the first time I saw an adorable young gentleman sitting on a grimy yellow sofa in a smoky Irish Pub. And my visions of a sharply dressed investigative reporter vanished the first time I opened the Our Town magazine and saw my travel feature and photos in print.

As for those ankle biters, well I don't even stand a chance with them. I am the totally dorky mom who broadcasts to the world the first time my child puts her pee pee in the potty as if she invented the entire concept of sitting on a toilet rather than copping a squat in a field. And the one in-utero can make me beam just by pouncing on my bladder.

So come June, I might squeeze my chunky butt into some braggin' pants and mosey on out to Texas after all. I've got plenty to be proud of and plenty that I've accomplished that my fellow classmates need to know about.

Plus I know from Facebook stalking that my high school arch nemesis and ultra-popular mean girl got pregnant out of wedlock and is really fat now. So at least I can give one condescending smile while I'm there. I'm going.

Creepy and Proud

It's amazing what a perfect parent I was before I actually had children. I had such a firm idea of what my offspring would and would not do and the lengths I'd go to, to ensure that I was not this or that kind of parent. So I guess I understand a little bit about the heat I've taken lately for breastfeeding my toddler. I have to admit that pre-parenthood I too scoffed at the women who nursed their youngin's past a year. I think I even used the word "creepy" to describe it. And so naturally parental karma has come back to bite me, and I find myself a very creepy, very wrong nursing mother.

Before the idea of parenthood was a blip on my radar, I was actually sicked out by nursing moms everywhere. I remember ushering my cousin to the bathroom when her newborn baby got hungry one evening, while we were all trying to enjoy a nice meal at the Barn Door Steakhouse.

This lovely West Texas treasure was just too fine an establishment for her to go trashing it up by unnecessarily exposing herself. Oh no, instead I whisked her past the corral of mullets and press-on fingernails to the bathroom where she couldn't disrupt anyone's dinner. And I tolerated her choice to feed her kid on the bench inside the bathroom rather than hide away in the stall. I just made sure to stand in front of her in case someone came into the restroom. They deserved to potty in peace without being exposed to such vulgarity. And she obliged. She hid in the bathroom like some sort of deviant with a secret.

But even as I matured and realized that this was a natural and necessary part of motherhood, I still held some high-and-mighty beliefs about how long this nursing bit should go on. I was pregnant with my baby girl, and that same cousin of mine was nursing her 18-month-old son.

Well I'm so glad that I know everything, because I kindly told her that it was time to wean him, seeing as how he could ask for seconds and all. How good of me to let this mother of two, soon to be mother of three, know how to appropriately parent. And what a noble deed I did by informing her of the right time to wean her child. I remember the knowing smile she gave me as she told me that he just wasn't ready.

"But, but you're 3 months pregnant, and he's 18 months, and he's old. And there's no reason. And it's ridiculous," I scoffed.

The whole family just knew she needed to give it up. Someone said she was just doing it for herself. She didn't want her baby to grow up, and she couldn't face the fact that he wasn't a baby anymore. Another person said she was just too soft. She needed to stand up to that kid and show him who was boss.

I believe my mother was the only person who told us all to shut up. My mother, a woman who formula fed both her children from day one, told us all to mind our own beeswax. She especially told me to butt out, and to just wait until I had my own kids.

Well silly mother, I thought. What did she know? I knew exactly what I was going to do. I would nurse my child until they had been on this earth exactly 365 days. Maybe I would give her 366 days. Let her enjoy her birthday. But the day after she turned one, the party would be over.

I wasn't some weak parent who couldn't tell her child no. My dear husband and I smugly discussed the fact that you simply had to put your foot down in a situation like that. After all, it's your will against that of a child. How silly that some parents can't just stand firm. Pish posh. That certainly wouldn't be the case with us.

Mmmm. You know I've learned that if you put a little sugar on them, those pre-parenting words are a little easier to swallow. My little monkey is 15 months, and shows no sign of weaning at the moment. And maybe I don't hate the fact that I still get an extra 600 free calories a day to do with what I please. And I'm sure there would be quite a scene the first time I tried to deny her milk. But those certainly aren't the real reasons I've chosen to be a creepy toddler nurser.

No, like many other "terrible" choices I've made as a mother, this one just works for us. Because she's allergic to cow's milk I'd have to try and wean her off of me and onto soymilk or some alternative.

Now let's see, my milk is more nutritious, it's free, and it's quite portable. It's also a surefire way to get her to nap. It's a lifesaver when she's teething. It ensures that I maintain a healthy diet, so that she's getting the best nutrition possible. Not to mention the wicked case of mastitis that will inevitably ensue, should I decide to just cut her off one day. She's happy and healthy, and so am I. So why the stigma?

Why was it the right thing to do at 11 months and 364 days, but horrifying at 12 months 1 day? And why is it creepy for my child to drink my milk, but it's the social norm for kids to drink milk from another animal? I just don't understand how what I'm doing is "unnatural" and "gross". But if I give her processed milk from another species, that is "normal".

Now don't get me wrong. I plan to stop one day. I don't intend to give her milk breaks in kindergarten. I think once it interferes with her social life, I'll throw in the towel. And really I'm hoping that she'll decide to give it up before it comes to that. But for now I'll just take it one creepy day at a time.

Because if I've learned anything about parenting karma it's that the only thing you know for sure about the future is that you don't know anything at all.

Farewell to a Friend
This award winner is near and dear to my heart.

I had an interesting week as a parent. I learned that a toilet will have no problem eating a pair of Minnie Mouse underpants without even a hint of indigestion or regret. I learned that any toy in the store will be put happily back on the shelf as long as it has its Mommy and Daddy, a.k.a. other toys that look similar. And I learned that explaining death to a toddler can be one of the most difficult, soul-wrenching, yet therapeutic gifts of motherhood.

I lost a very dear friend this week. She was a four-legged little fur ball I've had since high school. Cuddles was half cat half debutante trapped in a poodle body. I didn't ask for the little curly top. When my mom said she was going to get us a dog I begged for a Shar Pei.

But when she brought home our little Cuddles I couldn't help but love her. She looked like a tiny lamb no bigger than a cantaloupe, but twice as sweet. The little cotton ball just seemed to float over the floors and all you could see were two little black dots peering up at us, and a tiny black nose peeking out of the fluff. She was the snuggliest little ball of puffery that ever lived.

It was assumed she'd be the family dog, but once she was home, she was my dog. She slept in my room. She followed me around the house. She was my little companion.

On my 18th birthday I moved into my first apartment, and she snuggled into the crook of my legs the first night I spent alone. I felt protected by all five pounds of her. When I left Texas to head to college in Florida, the dorm had a strict policy against canine companions. So I said goodbye to my little pal, promising to see her at Thanksgiving.

It was a miracle she survived. My mom called to tell me that Cuddles wouldn't eat and just sat on the couch staring out the door like she was waiting for me to come home. I went out that day to look for a place to rent that was four-legged friendly. I found one the same week I found the man I would marry.

And she was there for that too. She was there for me the night before my wedding when I had the jitters. I had to cover my toes because she was going to lick them clean off my feet. She always knew when I needed a little reassurance.

I took her with me when I moved into my first house with my new husband. With my whole family back in Texas, she was my baby and my closest relative for the first four years of our marriage. And when I lost my first pregnancy and my first chance at a real baby, her silent comfort saw me through.

About a year later, when I brought my daughter home from the hospital, she was there waiting in anticipation. I watched apprehensively, wondering what she would think of this new little life I'd brought into the house. Cuddles was always very protective of me, and could get pretty jealous at times. I hoped that the transition wouldn't be too rough.

But she took one sniff of that baby and knew that she was a little part of me. They were best pals from day one. Cuddles never barked or became annoyed with Sunny's crying or curious tugs at her ears. It might have been because with that baby around Cuddles got a lot more fallen table scraps.

She let a lot of Sunny's behavior slide. She was almost 10 when Sunny was born, so her old age didn't leave room for much frolicking or playing. But every once in a while she'd get a burst of energy and prance around delighting my daughter.

And Sunny was absolutely in love. When we left the house she wanted to be the one to put Cuddles in her kennel. And when we were gone she asked to go home to see her. I once asked her where is home and she said "With Mommy and Daddy and Cuddles."

So the night she passed, I wasn't just sad that I'd lost a friend. But I dreaded having to try and explain her absence to a 2-year-old who adored her. I was furious that I had to put her through this, and I was angry that I'd let myself get so attached to something with such a short life span.

The next morning, Sunny bounded out of her room and before breakfast was served she said "Just second Mommy. I need let Cuddles go potty."

It was time. I had to explain to my toddler that her little pal was gone.

"Sweety, Cuddles was old. And sometimes, when dogs are old they die," I told her. We thought it would be best to be direct.

"Where Cuddles Mommy?" she asked. "I want Cuddles."

"Well she's gone Sweetheart, so that means we can't hold her anymore. But we can see her in pictures," I told her biting back tears.

"Oh," she said. And she was quiet for a while.

Then she said with a smile, "I like Cuddles Mommy. And Cuddles like me."

Without the concept of time and the questions of the afterlife, my little toddler was just happy to have known such a great little friend. It made me realize how lucky I was to have had such a great friend to be there for me when I needed her all those years.

Sunny still talks about Cuddles all the time, and sometimes it's with a little sadness because she's gone. But it's always good memories that she shares with me. And it makes me so grateful that our friend was able to leave such beautiful little paw prints in our hearts.

Wildflowers and Weeds

I was 5, and it was a sunny spring day in West Texas when I found a cluster of tiny white flowers among the dust and sticker burrs of my native landscape. They were so beautiful with their sturdy green stems and delicate white tear drop leaves. I plucked them carefully out of the ground and ran across the yard to show my grandmother my new treasures.

As I bounded in the house my great aunt shrieked, "Get those weeds out of here! I can't breathe." Aunt Darla always had a flair for the dramatic. A chain smoker since she was about 9 years old, she had trouble breathing when people were wearing deodorant.

The smile faded from my face as I looked at the little bouquet. These couldn't possibly be weeds. Weeds were a nuisance; something unwanted and invasive. How could such a tiny burst of beauty be an intrusion on that stark and dusty landscape?

My grandmother told her sister to hush and grabbed a small empty jelly jar. She filled it with a little water and placed my tiny bouquet in gently. She displayed the arrangement prominently on the kitchen table, so I beamed and ran outside. Aunt Darla couldn't take the fumes and had to leave.

I later asked my grandmother if those flowers were in fact weeds. She paused for a moment and asked me if I thought they were.

I said no way.

The whole yard was dry dirt. There were painful sticker burrs and fire ant hills dotting the landscape. I got tangled in tumbleweeds as I ran across the dusty yard. These little white flowers seemed so full of life. They were sturdy enough to survive the harsh conditions of the desert, but they were so delicate and pretty that they stood out among the browns and tans of the land I spent roaming as a child.

Grandma said every year in spring people trek to South Texas to watch the bluebonnets bloom. The medians and vacant fields are flooded with a sea of blue, then orange swirls when the Indian paintbrushes come to life. Then as more wildflowers bloom the pink, purple, yellow and red hues paint the landscape. People pull off the highway to snap pictures of their babies nestled among the wildflowers, and families meet photographers in fields to get professional photos taken with them. But in all actuality these wildflowers are weeds. They aren't planted like pansies or roses, but instead they grow wild each year just like crab grass or sticker burrs.

But they're an annual sign of spring. They've become a Texas tradition. You can't even get a Texas driver's license without presenting proof of residency with a bluebonnet photo and a passing grade on your Alamo factoid quiz.

My grandmother explained that because of a collective agreement, those wildflowers are deemed valuable. They aren't weeds because so many people can see their beauty. I asked if she thought my flowers were beautiful. Of course she said yes.

My grandmother taught me that the difference between weeds and flowers is perspective. There are plenty of things in our lives that just pop up. They seem like a nuisance because they are unexpected and different than everything we are used to. But we can make a choice to see these unexpected little blessings as flowers instead of weeds. It's all in the way we look at them.

I watched my 4-year-old daughter pluck a dandelion from the grass outside of her school. Instinctively she closed her blue eyes and blew the fluffy seeds into the wind. I asked if she made a wish, and she giggled and said yes. She whispered that she wished for more dandelions.

I smiled knowing that those little floating seeds were all potential dandelions carrying her wish across the sky. They would soon land, and some of them would in fact make her wish come true.

I'm sure whoever was in charge of keeping the grounds of her preschool would see those future dandelions as a nuisance. A weed to be eradicated. But to my daughter they were a wish come true, and I for one can see the beauty in that.

Working Mothers

Each morning in the a.m. I wake up in my sleeping bed. I brush my mouth teeth with my toothbrush and fix some kind of food breakfast for eating. I clean my living-in house and get in my driving car to run my errands. All the while I have a little child kid attach glued to my hip waist.

Sorry if I seem a little bit redundant or like I'm adding too many unnecessary adjectives that don't need to be added to words because they aren't necessary for you to understand the words they're being added to, forgive me and I'm sorry. But I've heard the term "working mother" used a lot recently, and I've gotten a little perturbed at the definition of working.

First let me issue a very heartfelt shout out to those mothers who must leave their offspring in the care of others while they work outside the home on a 9-to-5 daily basis. Bless their hearts because I know leaving my little 'un for even half an hour at the gym daycare was painful. So I do want to commend them for their bravery.

There are all sorts of crackpots taking care of kids out there, and I know what kind of mischief my angel can conjure when she's right under my very watchful eye. So for those who have no choice but to entrust their young ones to someone else for several hours each day, I truly do have much respect.

And even those who choose to go back to work, or those who have a stay-at-home husband still face their own set of challenges. I'm not in their position, but I would imagine it's tough for any mom to leave her children at one point or another. And she still has to drag her booty out of bed early each morning and put on a professional face after being up all night with her little darling. So there are hardships all around.

But I must admit, at times I am awfully jealous of that woman dragging her booty out of bed. You see the first day of leaving the tiny one I'm sure is hard. If they're not old enough to notice that you're gone and scream and wail in protest, I'd be willing to bet it's still nerve-wracking to release them into the care-taker's arms for the first time. Some moms even break down in hysterics, call it quits their first day back on the job, and try again another day. You know who you are.

But once it is confirmed that the caregiver is not only capable of sustaining the life of the child, but also enriching their life and bringing a smile to said child's face, well then I think it gets a little easier. And it's at that point I'm green with envy.

You see, my B.S. in Journalism isn't a degree that has CEOs beating down my door with million dollar salary offers in hand. Shocker. And my pre-baby take-home pay would have barely covered the cost of child care. So the unanimous decision in the Henry household was that I would stay home to bear and rear our youngin's. Well the decision for me to bear them was not exactly left up to me, but the hubby's not really into experimental medicine of that nature. So I'm stuck with that one.

Nonetheless, I did the deed, grew the child, popped her out and then quit my job to raise her. And she's really a swell kid, and I do have the privilege of witnessing all the wonders that she brings each day. But I've got to tell you it's no walk in the park. I don't feel like I'm a "vacationing mother", and I can assure you that my day is very much full of what I consider "work."

I would kill for a space of my own to get things done. Even a bitty tiny cubicle sounds like heaven. Instead I feel like a border collie wrangling and herding the kid away from the open dishwasher, fireplace, stairs and other hazards. Oh barricades you say? We don't call them baby gates in this house. Those are deadly climbing ladders and are classified under "Things you wouldn't think I could hurt myself with but oh were you wrong."

And maybe I'm part Lab since I'm often panting and chasing her through the house trying to retrieve the armfuls of laundry I JUST folded or my cell phone and car keys that like to go swimming in the toilet. All I know is at the end of my "work" day (wait when does my day end?) I'm dead dog tired.

And oh what I wouldn't give for a lunch break. I don't want to sound whiny, because I'm so grateful that I'm able to stay home and bond and share special moments and once in a very blue almost purple moon sneak in a quick afternoon nap when I accidentally stop moving for a second. But those busy heroic Super Moms who work a Nine-to-Fiver outside the home get a break from their kids. And when they get home after a hard day at the office, they are greeted by a little tyke who is oh so happy to see them again. My kid sees me all day and every once in a while I swear she looks at me like "Ugh you again? Don't you have somewhere to be?"

Well it's certainly not the bank seeing as how I get no paycheck. I miss that as well because it was physical evidence that I was doing something someone appreciated. Now I'm sure when my own little darling is a super genius, well-rounded adult with children of her own she'll call me at least once a day to thank me for the one-on-one attention. But until then my wages will come in the form of sweet giggles, the privilege to witness first steps and first words first-hand, and the self-reassurance that I can take some of the credit for her learning the color red.

So although I don't have an office, a salary and some days don't even bother to put on real pants, I still consider myself a very hard working mom.

Bye Bye Baby

I heard the most beautifully sad song today. It wasn't a twangy country tune, or a slow-dance ballad. It's one you probably know, and it's one I learned as a child. It goes, "Happy birthday to you. Happy birthday to you. Happy birthday dear so and so. Happy birthday to you."

Typically this song is only upsetting for those celebrating the 10th anniversary of their 30th birthday. But when the "so and so" was replaced by my baby girl's name, this song put a knot in my throat and a tear in my eye.

And the second verse, "How oh-old are you? How oh-old are you? How old are you Sunny? How oh-old are you?" Well that one just opened the water works.

So much so that the third verse, "She's wuh-un year old. She's wuh-un year old. She's wuh-un year old. Sunny's wuh-un year old," well that one was an unrecognizable stream of blubbering sniffles.

My baby is one. It's just not possible. Only a second ago I was toting her around all safe and warm in my womb. She'd tumble and somersault while I read books about What to Expect. And I had read all the books, so I thought I knew just what to expect. But oh, what a year of surprises this has been.

The first thing I didn't expect was how big my love could be for something that small. It's not that I didn't think I'd love her with my whole heart. It's just that I didn't know how big my heart would grow to be. I wouldn't just take a bullet for this kid. I'd take the bullet and get back up to stomp the face of the person who even though about putting such a dangerous object within 100 yards of my precious angel.

They also don't tell you that the world changes once that child arrives. Oh people can tell you all day how different your life will be once you have a child. But until that little miracle arrives, you just think that means you won't be going to the movies for a while.

But no.

When Sunny was born, the world I used to know vanished. I remember being wheeled out of the hospital as Cary pulled the car around. And as I looked up at the sky, the air smelled different. It's as if when I waddled my pregnant butt through those revolving doors, I was entering a black hole. And as I came out of the same doors a few days later, I was entering a parallel universe.

That has to be what it is. The Parents and the Non-Parents co-exist in different layers of the universe.

Everything looks the same, but it's different. We can see the Non-Parents, and they can see us. They can especially see us when our children are screaming bloody murder in a fine family dining establishment. But there's some sort of layer between us.

When I lived in the NP world, I was a thrill junkie. I loved riding roller coasters and watching scary movies. I craved the adrenaline rush. But now that I've entered the Parenting world, my adrenaline is jacked up nearly all day. I'm chasing this little thing around who likes to dive off of beds and literally play with fire. And it's my sole job to make sure she lives to see another day. Any more adrenaline rushes would send me into cardiac arrest.

So although I used to curl up in the dark and enjoy a good thriller, I now leave the lights on just a little bit during Finding Nemo. I can feel for that little clown fish father, and I hope that my baby never gets scooped up by a scuba diver dentist with a deranged niece.

But of all the things I didn't expect, I think the one that shocked me the most is the fact that I'd have to say goodbye so soon. When I found out I was pregnant, I knew that someday I'd have to fight back tears as we moved her into her college dorm. And I knew I wouldn't be able to stop the tears when her daddy walked her down the aisle. But I never imagined that I'd only have a year before I had to say my first goodbye.

Yep, just one year after I gave birth to the most beautiful creature on earth, I had to say goodbye to Baby Sunny.

You see as we sang the words, "Happy birthday to you," I realized that Baby Sunny was slipping away, and Toddler Sunny was moving in with us. My first clue should have been the disappearance of the 3-month onesies and the breast pump, but I was oblivious until I heard, "How oh-old are you?"

As we all know, at wu-uhn year old, she's not a baby anymore. She's a walking, talking trouble machine, who is slowly gaining the independence I desperately desired just 11 months ago.

Baby Sunny needed me for everything. I was her source of transportation, food, entertainment and security. I was on call for that child 24 hours a day and seven days a week. But Toddler Sunny just waddles her way over to her box of teething biscuits and giggles as she dumps them on the floor for a feast. My job has been reduced to security detail. I just have to make sure she doesn't smack her head into anything as she masters this walking business. And truth be told, I might be fired soon from that.

I remember thinking when she was just a few weeks old, and I was sleep deprived and hormonal as all get out, that if I could just stick it out until she was a little more self-sufficient it would get easier. I felt guilty for wishing that she didn't need me for everything. And now that she doesn't, I feel a little remorse for not cherishing every single solitary screaming moment of those first few months.

Because now that Baby Sunny is gone, all I have left of her is a hard drive full of photos and videos that I don't have time to peruse because Toddler Sunny is trying to ride the poodle around the living room.

But I have to say, as I'm starting to get to know Toddler Sunny, I think I have more in common with her than I did with Baby Sunny. Toddler Sunny gets my sense of humor, and she understands way more English.

She's a giggly little squirt with a mischievous grin and a penchant for cuddling. And although she doesn't need me to do everything for her, she certainly wants me around to watch her do it for herself. We're going through a phase now where she crawls up my leg if I try to put her down too soon. She loves me with her whole heart, and she's just so darn fun. I feel a little guilty because although Baby Sunny was so sweet, Toddler Sunny is the one I want to party with. The little bouncy butt jig she does when she hears music is just about the cutest thing I've ever seen.

So I'll say goodbye to Baby Sunny with a tear in my eye. But I will welcome the birth of Toddler Sunny. She's spunky, and inquisitive and someone I love discovering the world with. She loves to point and make a sound as if to say "What's that Mommy?" She's just a little sponge soaking up all I can teach her.

And since she loves to dance and sing, I'll teach her a little ditty I learned as a kid.

"Happy birthday to you. Happy birthday to you. Happy birthday Toddler Sunny. Happy birthday to you."

Squirrels Will Be Squirrels

It all started with that blasted squirrel. A few weeks ago the Hubs noticed some insulation missing in the attic. He grabbed some foam from Home Depot and got to work filling in the holes. As he was spraying the insulation he was suddenly blasted in the face by a tiny baby squirrel bursting through the foam launching himself to freedom.

Unfortunately Skitters didn't know that foam insulation starts out as foam and quickly turns into rock hard plastic. So here we are with this teensy squirrel baby covered head to toe in what will soon become an exoskeleton.

I am a serious bleeding heart animal lover. I always knew I'd be the crazy cat lady living in the country with all the stray animals. Like a Disney princess, but with a lot less singing. But upon having children I noticed that all my nurturing mojo was used up daily by 3:30 p.m., so I no longer yearned for a barnyard full of critters.

However, this was a baby squirrel who was facing certain death because of man-made goop applied by my husband. I felt some responsibility to help this poor creature. So here I was dusting off our little cat carrier to rush a baby squirrel to a wildlife rescue in town. I would just drop the critter off and know I did the right thing.

Apparently doing the right thing isn't always rewarded with candy kisses and a pat on the back because as I took my exit only 10 minutes away from the wildlife rescue I see flashing lights in my rearview mirror. The officer briskly asked for my license and bolted off to write me a citation before I could explain that I was in the midst of a life or death situation.

As he presented me with a hefty speeding ticket I asked where the wildlife rescue was and explained my story. He probably contemplated testing my blood alcohol level as he peeked in the back window to see if I indeed had a tiny plastic squirrel in the cat carrier. The guy felt bad once he realized why I was speeding, but the ticket had already been issued, so his hands were tied. I quickly signed off saying I'd show up in court, and I was on my way once again to save this ridiculous rodent.

Before reaching the rescue I got lost in the absolute scariest part of town I've ever been in, my preschooler decided she needed to pee and my toddler threw up. It was a magical rescue to say the least.

At one point Sunny piped up from the back and said "Mom, you got a ticket, we're lost in the ghetto and the squirrel is probably dead. I think this is where our story ends."

As I bit back tears I explained that we were almost there and we had to press on because we don't quit. Minutes later we did make it to the sanctuary. We dropped off the little fella with a semi-hopeful prognosis from the rescue volunteers.

But as I drove home, I was cursing under my breath. I tried to rescue that snake food and all I got was a huge ticket, my car smelled like barf and we didn't even know if Skitters would survive. Sunny asked why I was so frazzled. I explained that I didn't know how I was going to tell Daddy that I just got a $150 speeding ticket trying to rescue a glorified rat.

"Just hide it under your seat Mommy," she said very seriously. "Daddy won't find it under there."

I choked back a chuckle and explained that Mommy doesn't hide things from Daddy and that I would just have to tell him about it because it was the right thing to do. She was quiet for a while, and then she said "Mommy when I am a grown up I will always do the right thing."

I told her I was glad to hear it, and then it dawned on me why I felt compelled to try and save this creature that was hardly a speck in the food chain. Because it was right. And as my baby grows up she'll be faced with choices in life to help someone in need, to quit when things get tough or to tell the truth. And I hope in those moments she might think back to our squirrel rescue and remember to do what is right.

That being said I will be checking under her car seat tomorrow. I'm almost afraid to know what she's squirreled away down there.

A Little Sisterly Advice

I spent the weekend holed away in a rental house in the mountains with my in-laws. Sounds like a column that writes itself, but sadly my mother-in-law and father-in-law are awesome.

My mother-in-law is a clean freak, but she has learned to love me filth and all. And my father-in-law is wildly inappropriate at times, but it's why I love him. However, in the eight years we've been married I haven't spent a ton of time with my brother-in-law and his wife. This weekend we got super cozy.

They got married the same summer we did, and I was overjoyed to have a sister. I'd grown up with a brother five years younger, and while we're best friends now, and he was a good sport about wearing my slips and hair bows, he was really a poor substitute for a sister.

Shelly also grew up with one younger brother, but I guess he looked better in drag because she never really seemed as jazzed about the idea of having a sister as I was. And so we never bonded over painted toenails or giggled like schoolgirls on a shopping trip. No, my girly void wasn't filled until I had my own beautiful daughters.

Now these two fine young people are only two years my senior, but like many folks of my generation they postponed having children to focus on having a career and a life. My Hubs and I dove right in at the ripe ol' age of 25. Middle-aged if we lived in the 1920s, but practically babies by today's standards. But once my sis-in-law hit 30 she said they started thinking about repopulating.

I believe her exact words were "Yeah when I was in my 20s I was like 'Eww a baby, kill it.' But once I hit 30 it was like 'Aww, a baby.'" Spoken like a true mother.

The first thing they did was buy a "family" car. They've been through about eight new cars in the eight years they've been married, but more power to them. She's a math teacher, so they can figure out if that's financially a good idea.

At this point they had a 3-year-old mustang and a 1-year-old corvette. I know this because they got a car every time I had a baby. Naturally they needed something more family friendly than their race cars, so they traded in the mustang and got a souped-up sport racing edition of the Ford Focus. No need to give up your love of fast driving just because of a tiny baby. Yes you could fit an infant seat in the mustang, and no you can't in the corvette. But the corvette is faster, so it gets to stay. The perfect labor and delivery car. It's logic.

She also informed me that the reason they waited to have a baby is because they'd seen their friends who had babies young, and the child dictated their lives. Ehem no offense. They vowed never to be the parents who let a child decide what they can and can't do. They still wanted to take ski trips and go to the race track, and by golly no child is going to stop them. "The baby will just have to fit into our plans," she said confidently.

Now reader I did manage to hold my giggles. I'm sure North Face makes some sort of baby carrier so you can strap the infant to you while careening down a mountain. They have a noble notion about children that I find absolutely precious. They've got it all planned out down to the month they will conceive, so that the baby fits into their school schedule. No they won't be using any fertility methods, she is just super confident in her ability to control her uterus. So that's wonderful. I hope it works out for them.

They might very well have the little boy my father-in-law is desperate for. He will be a wonderfully well-behaved little gentleman: a stark contrast to my two wild women. He will wear little suits and say things like "Papa, may I please help Mother set the table? I'm ever so hungry for the delicious pheasant she has graciously prepared." And he'll not make eye contact out of reverence to his benevolent father.

But I also know about parenting karma. I should have told her the moment we started talking babies, but I got wrapped up in the excitement of having a niece or nephew. But someone should tell them about parenting karma. You never ever say aloud the things you will not do. The parenting gods are always on high alert for those who dare tempt them.

I said I would never let my kids sleep in my bed and never nurse a baby past one year. I ended up with an almost 2-year-old nursing herself to sleep every night. I learned though. I repented, never said any parenting blasphemy again and the gods gave me a reprieve with my second child.

But she broke the rule, and she said it aloud. She spoke all sorts of certainties about what the baby would and would not do and what sort of things she would not allow. So I will pray for her. Pray to the parenting gods to spare her for she knew not what she did. Pray that they are spared and that they have this well-behaved racetrack loving ski bunny.

Nah, maybe I'll just sit back and paint my little girls' piggies and giggle to myself. I guess she really should have taken me up on that shopping trip. I could have bestowed some sisterly advice.

Squirrel Milk

This is the extended story of my squirrel saga published on preschoolproblems.blogspot.com

So you know that moment when you're about to breast feed a baby squirrel? Well that was me yesterday.

It all started when Hubs found a nest in the nook in our roof. He went to spray insulation in the attic that had been torn out to make said nest, and while he's spraying a baby squirrel jumps through the foam. The poor bugger is covered in this hardening goop so Hubs traps him in a pillowcase. I rushed him to an animal sanctuary with a less than promising prognosis.

Later at home I am bawling in the laundry room over this little squirrel who might not survive when what do I see out the window but another baby squirrel. Just lying there trembling. Well I'm already in a state because of Skitters, so Hubs goes out to check on this one to see if he's hurt. Well little Chipper runs away to our ac unit barking at anyone who dares come near him. Oh and crying desperately for his mama.

Hubs has perspective. These are rodents who have the potential to set our house on fire by chewing wires etc. But all I see is a scared baby whose mama is probably worried sick, and I'm crushed.

I start trying to research how old these fuzz buckets are, and I decide they're about 8 weeks. They still need mama but will be evicted soon. Still I am concerned.

My natural instinct is to feed and warm him, but what can baby squirrels eat? Well I note that first and foremost they still take mama's milk. We don't keep cow's milk in the house because of Sweet Pea's sensitivity. She's still taking her mama's milk too.

So here we are friends. I'm a grown woman searching the house for my breast pump to play wet nurse to a baby squirrel.

There comes a point in every marriage where your loyalties are tested. And yesterday was that day. It's no secret that I'm a bit of a lactivist. I try to normalize breastfeeding by just doing it whenever and wherever my kid needs it. Not really to make a statement other than "look it's a boob. It's working. And it's not porn. And you don't have to stuff dollars in my bra (you can just set them on the bench)."

And with all his faults and for all the times Hubs acts like a real meat head, he has always been a huge supporter of the way I nourish our babies. He's the one who put the bumper sticker on my car that says "If my breast feeding offends you feel free to put a blanket over your head."

So rather than having me committed for trying to save a baby squirrel with human boob juice, he went on about his business trying to find little Chipper's mama.

I never found my pump, but he found Mama. And the next day I put Chipper's little bed of towels near mama's favorite tree and she found him.

I was telling this story to a friend and she was dying at the absurdity. But while I see the humor, I don't really see all the crazy? Isn't that what we as mothers should do? Help each other? There's so much judgment and competition between mothers now. Formula vs. breast milk. Natural birth vs. C-section. Rodent vs. human. We're all just mothers. We want to do the best WE can for our kids. Not what other moms can. But the best WE can as their mom. We want our kids to be strong and smart and the fastest kid on the soccer team. We want them to walk the earliest and talk before they turn 1 and read before they are 3 and color a picture of a bear like nobody's business.

But above all, as mothers we all want our children to feel happy, healthy and safe.

So that's what I did. I tried to keep another mother's baby safe. I didn't hand her a pamphlet about the benefits of human breast milk. Her squirrel milk is probably fine. I didn't judge her choice of bedding. Insulation is soft, so clearly those squirrel pups are just SIDS waiting to happen. Especially because I can only assume she *gasp* co-sleeps with them.

But I passed no judgment on that mama. Instead I looked out for her most precious gift. I had her back in her time of need. Maybe if we all committed to breast feeding a squirrel, the world might be a safer and more loving place. Bring back a sense of community to this harsh world.

Yeah I'll just be waiting in my room for the straight jacket. I'm about a size 5....Ok a 7. Don't judge me.

Finding My Why

On Sunday I met a fabulous couple. She works in human resources and has the most sparkly blue eyes on the planet. He is a super friendly military hero. They're one of those couples who are so deeply in love that you can't help but notice when one gently reaches for the other one's hand, or when they seem to communicate with just a subtle glance. The only thing that could distract you from their love for each other is the pain that crosses those baby blues when a young mother shuffles by carrying her newborn snuggled sweetly in his infant seat.

Years ago this sweet woman with the gentle smile lost the most primal right bestowed upon a woman. Cancer robbed her of the ability to bear her own children. The cancer is gone, but the yearning for a child remains.

As I sat across the table at a busy restaurant I listened as she and her husband told me their story. His eyes lit up as he talked about being a father, and she feigned a smile as she jokingly said she probably would make a terrible pregnant woman anyway. My husband squeezed my hand under the table.

I've talked about becoming a surrogate since the first time I gave birth. Pregnancy and childbirth have always fascinated me almost to the point of obsession. Once I got bit by the baby bug I was like a walking Wikipedia on pregnancy and childbirth. I wanted to know when the baby's heart would start beating or when it would grow eye lashes.

I lost my first pregnancy at 13 weeks. It was twins, and they'd stopped developing at 10 weeks. But my uterus totally let it go to voicemail when my body made the call. Instead of waking up cramping in the middle of the night, I found out at my 13 week checkup through a routine ultrasound.

I decided to wait a week to have another ultrasound just to be sure the twins weren't playing a terrible joke on me. It was pretty surreal and horrifying, but on April Fool's day the joke was over. The second ultrasound confirmed what we already knew, and I opted for surgery to expel the "products of conception" from my uterus.

I always hated that they called my babies products. They even threw away my ultrasound pictures because who wants pictures of some busted products?

I was completely devastated. I asked the doctor why they didn't make it. But he had no answers. I asked my mom why this happened to me. She said it was God's plan.

It took my strength not to fist fight my own mother over that comment. What sick plan would include this kind of pain? If God didn't want me to have kids then just don't let me get pregnant. Don't let me get my hopes up and then smash them into tiny little products of conception.

A month passed and I wasn't pregnant. Two months passed and I still got a big fat negative. Three. Four. At five months a friend of mine announced that she was accidentally pregs. I felt numb. Six months went by and another friend gently told me she was also pregnant. I feigned a smile, but she knew. We didn't talk about it as we walked through the book store. I tried to fake interest and put on the happy face. She always changed the subject. I was always grateful for the compassion she showed me. But the second I dropped her off I dissolved into a sobbing puddle of sadness.

We talked about adoption, but apparently there isn't actually this big playpen of tiny babies just waiting for a momma. Plus the thought of never having my own biological child was heartbreaking. I understand it seems selfish because there are orphans who need love. But I wanted my baby to get my Daddy's eyes or my husband's dimpled cheek.

Through my heartache I vowed that if I could just have a biological child of my own I would be forever grateful, and I would find a way to show it.

The next month I got a little pink line that changed my life. Nine months later my dear little Sunny was born, and two years after that I was pregnant with my sweet Violet.

I never understood why I had to suffer so much or why my babies were taken from me. I never understood why until I sat across that table this Sunday. I saw the same hurt and longing in her beautiful blue eyes.

And I found my why.

Away She Goes

Originally published in Our Town Magazine and on scarymommy.com

A new school year is upon us, and this year I get to enjoy the smell of a box of brand new crayons. My first-born fruit of my loins will be starting kindergarten this year, and thus begins such a bittersweet time.

My little Sunshine is a spunky spirited child whose antics delight me and simultaneously drive me to drink. She was the baby I couldn't leave at the gym daycare for more than 15 minutes because she screamed and clawed to try and reattach herself to my hip. I spent more time trying to squeeze into my yoga pants than I did actually swishing around on the elliptical machine. Every day I would get paged to come get my screaming child. Every day.

I cancelled my gym membership and vowed to hit the treadmill once again when she started preschool. Then I blinked, and it was time to enroll her. At this point she was 2, and I'd spent 821 days tending to her every need. This momma needed a break. I cleared my schedule the first day of school and planned to wait in the library. I knew they'd need me to come back to class and talk her down off her screaming ledge.

I hyped it up the whole way to school telling her how much fun she was going to have with all the new toys and friends. There was no way this little thing in the backseat even knew what I was babbling about, but I had to try. I needed a break.

As I posed her for a picture outside the church doors I got a little lump in my throat. Maybe she wouldn't scream for so long. Maybe she'd just cry a little and calm down after 15 minutes. I just wanted her first day to go well. I didn't have time to think about the fact that this was her first step away from me.

She didn't cry the first day. In fact I had to chase her into the classroom to get a goodbye kiss. That feeling of dread, that mommy guilt that was tugging on my heart telling me not to leave her and that she needed me just faded away. I was happy that she was happy.

Two days without my 2-year-old turned into three days without my 3-year-old, and as another year passed I found myself surfing job boards longing for the day that I'd go back to work full-time in a real big person office with big people chairs and quiet lunches. The terrible twos were nothing compared to the tyrannical threes, and I found myself just surviving motherhood one day at a time.

There were so many days that I looked around my filthy house and wished I had 5 minutes of peace. The sass that came out of my 3-year-old's mouth was atrocious and I had to remind myself that screaming at her would only teach her to scream. Instead I'd scream in my closet with the door shut and long for a shower without an audience.

Then the time came I realized my own mother was a dirty liar. She said 2 and 3 were really hard, but when they turn 4 they're angels. That advice stunk worse than my 1-year-old's diapers. Turns out 4 wasn't really much better than 3. It was battle after battle, day in and day out. She didn't want to wear anything purple, and only wanted to wear things with cats. She wasn't wearing those shoes because the buckle was too tight. Then it was too loose. Then it was too tight.

Every. Single. Day.

I spent more hours than I'd like to admit letting her watch marathons of Ruby Gloom on Netflix while I poured over job boards looking for freelance work. I yearned to be back in the land of rational people who were okay with anything other than chicken nuggets and boogers at lunch and who didn't wear jam as an accessory.

I scoffed at my friends who said they weren't ready to send their kids to all day kindergarten. I boasted that my kid was going to love it since she loves preschool so much. I tried to hide the fact that I was the one looking forward to a full day of productivity.

Then I blinked again. And as I registered my spunky sassy little girl for kindergarten I got another lump in my throat. What if she doesn't cry? What if I can't even catch her to give her a goodbye kiss? This magnificent and wonderful little creature that I created and spent 1,898 days with is taking another step away from me. Our special time together is over. And now I can't help but long for those days of jam smeared kisses. I regret the Netflix marathons and I know that I must savor these last few weeks that I have her all to myself.

It's heartbreaking, and wonderful and terrifying all at once. And I know that all I can do when I drop her off and the tears well up in my eyes is just try not to blink.

Afterword

As I wrap this up I hope you have enjoyed this real and open look into my world. My hope is to have shed the outer layers of pretention and reservation we all wear out into the world so that I could share the naturally flawed but often beautiful side of married life and parenting.

It isn't my intention for you to walk away with some profound appreciation for life. Nor do I expect you to streak out of your house baring it all. I only hope to have entertained you for a little while, and to maybe give you someone with whom to commiserate and celebrate this ridiculous season of life.

And to let you know that this is what life looks like when I get Naked.

Made in the USA
Monee, IL
04 July 2021